CW01020552

'THE SONS OF RE'

To see a genuine cartouche inscribed in a tomb or on a temple wall, on a statue, or on a Papyrus, stirs one's imagination. It is a living signature of an ancient king of Egypt. To read his name today is probably the greatest compliment one can pay him, - for surely he has thus achieved the immortality that he craved!

'THE SONS OF RE'

CARTOUCHES OF THE KINGS OF EGYPT

BY

JOHN ROSE

Art work by the author

JR-T

1985

Copyright © 1985. J. Rose.

No part of this publication may be reproduced or transmitted in any form or by any means, electronic or mechanical, including photocopy, recording, or any information storage and retrieval system, without permission in writing from the publisher.

British Library Cataloguing in Publication Data

Rose, John, 1933-
The sons of Re : cartouches of the kings of Egypt.
1. Decoration and ornament, Egyptian
2. Decoration and ornament, Ancient 3. Egypt——
Antiquities
I. Title
745.4'41 NK1190

ISBN 0-9510432-0-X

Printed and bound in Great Britain by Deanprint Ltd,
Stockport, Cheshire.

Published by JR-T
Croft, Warrington, Cheshire.

PREFACE

This book is intended to provide a convenient guide to the kings' names contained in cartouches found in their tombs, on their monuments and other Egyptian artifacts. It allows easy identification of the cartouche without any knowledge of the hieroglyphs whatsoever. A secondary aim of the book is to provide a succinct commentary on the relationship between the kingship and the mythology of Egypt and to give some relevant information on the major kings. I have included a sketch map of Egypt showing the places mentioned, to enable the reader to locate the king's capital and his burial place where known.

The idea for a work of this nature arose from my early study of Egyptology, when during a first visit to Egypt I found great inconvenience in identifying the royal names in various cartouches without searching through a multitude of texts. A later visit armed with the manuscript of this book proved extremely rewarding, enhancing both the knowledge gained and the pleasure of the visit.

The historical time span of the narrative part of the book was determined by a desire to limit its data to that related to the native Egyptian Pharaohs, hence the title 'The Sons of Re'. Nectanebo II of the 30th Dynasty was the last true Pharaoh of all Egypt, but over the dynastic era some foreign or para-Egyptian kings reigned. These kings, the later Persian and Greco-Roman rulers, and the contemporary kings of Nubia, were thus pretenders to the 'Son of Re' title. I have included examples of their cartouches in order to distinguish them from those of the true Egyptian kings. I have likewise included a comprehensive selection of the Queens, Princes and Princesses, who also had their names in a cartouche, and cartouches of the early mythical god-kings.

In my registers of kings, I have included names known only from the historical Kings Lists as well as those that have been attested by the monuments and other inscriptions. Many kings' names from the historical lists have not yet been found on the monuments and some from the monuments are not found on the historical lists. I have included a brief description of the Kings Lists, and a copy of the classical list of the historian Manetho, it being the only one covering the whole historical span of the Pharaohs.

The chronology of the kings of Egypt is fraught with many difficulties, various authorities assigning different dates to both the start of the dynastic period and to the actual reigns of the kings. I felt that a practical solution would be to base my chronology on those widely known 'accurate' dates and on computations which I consider gave realistic minimum antiquity for the remainder. Although dates of the early kings of the 12th Dynasty and of kings from the 26th Dynasty on are known to be accurate, all other dates are approximate, with possibly a margin of error of up to 200 years for the commencement of the first dynasty. Dates of the New Kingdom reigns are more accurate but are not known with precision. My registers are thus founded on the Kings Lists where possible, otherwise following basically the sequences given by the authorities from my select bibliography. They are not intended to be definitive chronologies, but rather serve only to indicate to the reader the approximate dates when the kings reigned.

In researching, every opportunity has been seized to collect and verify as many cartouches as possible, visiting Egypt and many museums for this purpose. I am indebted, however, to the many Egyptologists, archaeologists and historians whose works I have also studied in my efforts to check and cross-reference the cartouches and the data on the kings.

I would like to acknowledge the help and tolerance shown by my wife Delyth and my daughter Julie during the research and compilation of this book. To the many friends and colleagues who have constantly encouraged me in my task, I also give my most sincere thanks.

CONTENTS

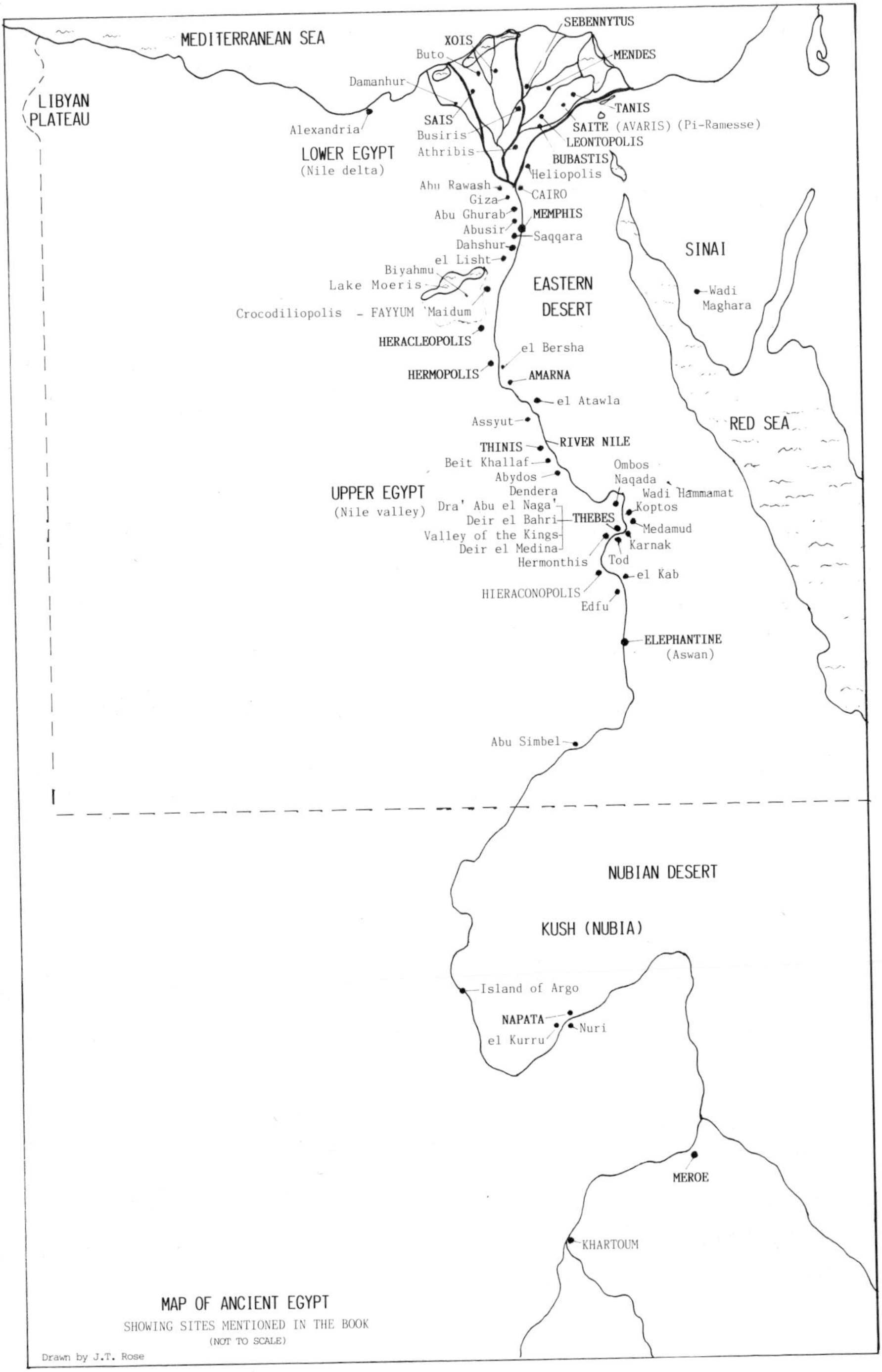

MAP OF ANCIENT EGYPT
SHOWING SITES MENTIONED IN THE BOOK
(NOT TO SCALE)

1 KINGS AND CARTOUCHES

Succession to the throne of Egypt usually passed through the female line, but the devine birth of the Pharaoh was essential to maintain his claim as the Son of Re. The majority of kings succeeded to the reign by birth and marriage to the heiress-queen. In a few cases a queen took the reign herself and became Pharaoh in her own right. A new dynasty was sometimes started by a usurper of the throne.

Most kings had five names. The first, the HORUS name, was borne by him as the earthly representative of the great Sky-God Horus. The name was placed within a rectangular shaped frame called a serekh,  prefixed by a hawk, the symbol of Horus.

The second, the TWO LADIES name  (Nebti), represents acceptance of him as lord of Upper and Lower Egypt by the two goddesses - Nekhebet the vulture goddess of Upper Egypt, and Edjo the cobra goddess of Lower Egypt.

The third, the GOLDEN HORUS name,  (Hor nub), represents the king as being of gold like the God Horus.

The names following each of the above titles are epithets referring to the king's position as a god.

The other two names refer to the king himself and are contained in a CARTOUCHE which is shaped like an oval, with a short vertical bar at one end. In detail the cartouche represents a knot of double thickness of rope, looped to be never ending, which may symbolise the all-embracing rule of the Pharaoh. 

The first cartouche name, called the PRENOMEN or throne name, is the name taken by the king on his ascension to the throne or coronation. It usually contains a statement about the Sun-God Re, sometimes with other epithets. The first cartouche is prefixed by the title "King of Upper and Lower Egypt". 

The second cartouche name, called the NOMEN, is the king's birth or family name which was sometimes combined with another epithet, prefixed by the title 'Son of Re'. 

The full use of two cartouche names started after the 4th Dynasty, the king, with few exceptions, taking the official throne name upon ascension. In pre-4th Dynasty reigns the king was represented mainly by his Horus name. Both the prenomen and nomen cartouches are shown in this book and some pertinent comments on each king are included. Although a complimentary Horus name is shown where known, it should be noted that many kings had numerous Horus names. Thus the Horus name alone might not serve to identify the king, the complimentary cartouche name will also be needed. Some kings took the name of their predecessors and thus for the proper identification of these kings both their prenomen and nomen are needed. In these cases the cartouche page has a cross-reference to the other kings with the same name. This enables the correct combination of the two cartouche names to be located, and a positive identification to be made, via these or via the king's Horus name.

Although the main titles prefixing the cartouches of the king were 'King of Upper and Lower Egypt' and 'Son of Re', sometimes these titles were replaced with others having the same meaning, or some other epithet such as 'Beautiful God' or 'Good God'. Sometimes the consort queen and other royal persons had their names within a cartouche. These cartouches are prefixed by a different title indicating the status of the person. A list of these alternative prefixes is included so that the reader may give credence to the cartouche being read.

As found in Egyptian scripts, in tombs, or on monuments, the cartouche may be lying horizontally or standing vertically and the hieroglyphs may be read from right to left or left to right, and top to bottom, depending upon the cartouche position in relation to the script or artifact upon which it is placed. In common with other hieroglyphic writings, the direction of the reading is indicated by the direction in which the animate objects face, ie, the hieroglyphs read in the direction towards the facing animate objects. For symmetry, all the royal cartouches in this book are shown lying horizontally and the reading is from left to right. In all situations the cartouche is always read towards the bar at the end.

Identificaiton of a cartouche is easily and quickly achieved by means of the book's unique cartouche location system, which enables the royal name to be found and identified without any previous knowledge of hieroglyphs.

It should be noted that some kings had many variant cartouches. Their names often appeared in slightly different forms. Sometimes they were written with different, but equivalent meaning, hieroglyphic signs.

Eg.  = m, being replaced with  = m, in Amenemhet,

thus  becomes 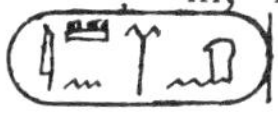

From the New Kingdom on, a variety of epithets were attached to the name within the cartouche. Sometimes these were varied for the same king, but the main elements of the name remained the same.

Sometimes a slightly different form of the epithet was attached to the name, eg.,  =  mery (beloved),

thus 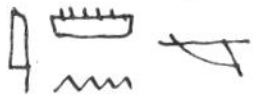 becomes 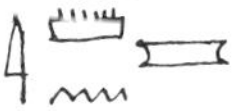 , etc.

Some of the variant epithets are shown in section 7, page 158.

To minimise the problem of variant cartouches, an alternative rendering of the name is shown above the cartouche. The reader will, with practice, be able to recognise the main elements of the name and be able to identify the name despite the variations.

The names of some of the mythical god-kings of Egyptian antiquity were later shown in cartouches and these are included and are shown standing vertically, to distinguish them from the cartouches of mortal kings. It should also be noted that the Egyptians sometimes placed the names of cities and of foreign countries in a form of cartouche. These names are easily distinguished by the serrated outline of the cartouche 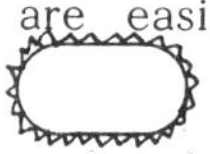 and the lack of a bar at the end.

The king's name may sometimes be found in connection with a place - temple, estate, district, town, or foreign country, etc. In this case the name is often placed within the sign for a mansion, or place of residence 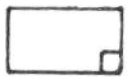 , or fortified place 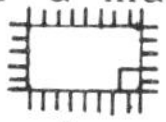 . The king's name can still be identified by applying the cartouche location system, but it should be noted that the name within the above frames may be merely that of the place or building, and will thus not be present in this book.

HONORIFIC TRANSPOSITION - In cartouches where the king's name is formed from a god's name, the god's name is usually written first out of respect, even though it is sometimes pronounced last.

2 THE KINGS LISTS

The ancient Egyptians believed that their kings were descended from devine beings who had earlier ruled over Egypt. In an 'Ancient Chronicle' they claimed that their antiquity spanned 36525 years, a great lunar/solar period which relates to the fabled rising of the dog-star Sirius. The chronicle claims 15 gods, 8 semi-gods and 30 dynasties of mortal kings. (Synecellus a Greek historian).

Other Greek writers gave lists of kings but the most informative of all came from Manetho, a High Priest of Egypt in the reign of Ptolemy II, 285-246 BC, who wrote a history of the ancient Egyptians, drawing up a list of kings commencing with seven dynasties of gods and semi-gods, followed by 30 dynasties of mortal kings ending with Nectanebo II. Later copiers of Manetho's list extended his 30 dynasties to include the Late Persian Period, ending with Alexander the Great, 332-323 BC.

Further historical kings lists have been found as follows:-

PALERMO STONE - A diorite block (now in Palermo Museum), which when complete contained the names of pre-dynastic kings of Lower and of Upper Egypt, followed by dynastic kings beginning with Menes and ending with kings of the 5th Dynasty.

ABYDOS LIST (1) - Limestone blocks from the temple of Ramesses II at Abydos (now in the British Museum), it shows cartouches, of which 34 survive in part or whole, of dynastic kings from Menes to Seti I and his son Ramesses II. When complete it was no doubt a duplicate of the list from the temple of Seti I, described below.

ABYDOS LIST (2) - Inscribed on the walls of the temple of Seti I at Abydos, it shows cartouches of 76 dynastic kings, beginning with Menes and ending with Seti I.

TABLET OF KARNAK - Inscribed in the temple of Amen-Re at Karnak in the reign of Tuthmosis III (now in the Louvre, Paris), it originally showed the cartouches of 61 dynastic kings - these however, were not disposed in chronological order.

As well as spanning from Menes to Tuthmosis III, it contains other dynastic kings not found on the Abydos or Saqqara lists.

TABLET OF SAQQARA - from the tomb of a royal scribe in the reign of Ramesses II (now in the Cairo Museum), it originally showed the cartouches of 58 dynastic kings, from Merpaba of the 1st Dynasty to Ramesses II.

TURIN CANON - This hieratic papyrus (now in the Turin Museum), dates from the 19th Dynasty and contained the cartouche names of pre-dynastic gods and demi-gods, and over 300 cartouche names of dynastic kings beginning with Menes and ending with the 17th Dynasty kings.

This papyrus was written in hieratic, not hieroglyphs and was badly damaged. It has been the source of the names and sequence of reign of many otherwise unknown kings not found in Manetho's list.

PRIEST LIST OF MEMPHIS - A list showing the sequence of the High Priests of Memphis, with the name of the king whose reign they served under. This list is damaged and therefore incomplete.

The above lists have been fairly well collaborated by detached monuments, but some names have still not been found, particularly from the Turin Canon. Apart from the two from Abydos, none of the lists are in complete accord, so it has not been possible to form a true chronological sequence from them.

I have endeavoured to show cartouches confirmed by the monuments, but where this has not been possible I have included those from the above lists.

MANETHO'S CLASSICAL KINGS LIST

(DERIVED FROM AFRICANUS)

DYNASTY OF GODS

Hephaestus
Helios
Agathodaemon
Cronos
Osiris and Isis
Typhon

DYNASTY OF DEMI-GODS

Orus
Ares
Anubis
Heracles
Apollo
Ammon
Tithoes
Sosus
Zeus

DYNASTIES OF KINGS

1ST DYNASTY – THINIS

Menes (62)	29
Athothis (57)	29
Kenkenes (31)	29
Uenephes (23)	30
Usaphaidos (20)	30
Miebidos (26)	30
Semempses (18)	31
Bieneches (26)	31

2ND DYNASTY – THINIS

Boethos (38)	32
Kaiechos (39)	32
Binothris (47)	33
Tlas (17)	33
Sethenes (41)	34
Chaires (17)	34
Nephercheres (25)	34
Sesochris (48)	35
Cheneres (30)	35

3RD DYNASTY – MEMPHIS

Necherophes (28)	36
Tosorthros (29)	36
Tyreis (7)	36
Mesochris (17)	36
Soyphis (16)	36
Tosertasis (19)	37
Aches (42)	37
Sephuris (30)	38
Kerpheres (26)	38

4TH DYNASTY – MEMPHIS

Soris (29)	41
Suphis (63)	41
Suphis (66)	42
Mencheres (63)	42
Ratoises (25)	41
Bicheris (22)	42
Sebercheres (7)	42
Thamphthis (9)	

5TH DYNASTY – ELEPHANTINE

Usercheres (28)	43
Sephres (13)	43
Nephercheres (20)	43
Sisires (7)	44
Cheres (20)	44
Rathures (44)	44
Mencheres (9)	45
Tancheres (44)	45
Onnus (33)	46

6TH DYNASTY – MEMPHIS

Othoes (30)	46
Phius (53)	47
Methusuphis (7)	47
Phiops (94)	47
Menthesuphis (1)	48
Nitocris (12)	48

7TH DYNASTY – MEMPHIS
70 who reigned for 70 days 51

8TH DYNASTY – 27 OF MEMPHIS
who reigned for 146 yrs 52

9TH DYNASTY – 19 KINGS OF
HERACLEOPOLIS for 409 yrs 52

10TH DYNASTY – 19 KINGS OF
HERACLEOPOLIS for 185 yrs 52
Achtoes 53

11TH DYNASTY – 16 KINGS OF
DIOSPOLIS for 43 yrs plus
Ammenemes (16) 58

12TH DYNASTY – DIOSPOLIS

Sesonchosis (46)	58
Ammanemes (38)	59
Sesostris (48)	59
Lachares (8)	60
Ameres (8)	60
Ammenemes (8)	60
Scemiophris (4)	61

13TH DYNASTY – 60 KINGS OF
DIOSPOLIS for 453 yrs 64

14TH DYNASTY – 76 KINGS OF
XOIS for 184 yrs 74

15TH DYNASTY – PHOENICIA (HYKSOS)

Saites (19)	77
Bnon (44)	77
Pachnan (61)	77
Staan (50)	77
Archles (49)	79
Aphophis (61)	78

16TH DYNASTY – 32 HYKSOS
KINGS for 518 yrs 79

17TH DYNASTY – 43 SHEPHERD
KINGS AND 43 THEBAN KINGS
for 151 yrs 81

18TH DYNASTY – THEBES

Amos	90
Chebros (13)	91
Amenophthis (24)	90
Amensis (22)	91
Misaphris (13)	91
Misphragmuthosis (26)	92
Tuthmosis (9)	92
Amenophis (31)	92
Orus (37)	93
Acherres (32)	93
Rathos (6)	94
Chebres (12)	
Acherres (12)	95
Armesis (5)	95
Ramesses (1)	95
Amenophath (19)	

19TH DYNASTY – DIOSPOLIS

Sethos (51)	96
Rapsaces (66)	96
Ammenephthes (20)	96
Ramesses (60)	96
Ammenemnes (5)	97
Thuoris (7)	98

20TH DYNASTY – 12 KINGS OF
DIOSPOLIS for 135 yrs 98

21ST DYNASTY – TANIS

Smendes (26)	110
Psusennes (46)	110
Nephercheres (4)	110
Amenophthis (9)	111
Osochor (6)	111
Psinaches (9)	111
Psusennes (14)	112

22ND DYNASTY – BUBASTUS

Sesonchis (21)	112
Osorthon (15)	112
3 other kings (25)	113
Takelothis (13)	114
3 other kings (42)	115

23RD DYNASTY – TANIS

Petubates (40)	116
Osorcho (8)	117
Psammus (10)	
Zet (31)	117

24TH DYNASTY – SAIS

Bochchoris (6)	120

25TH DYNASTY – ETHIOPIA

Sabacon (8)	126
Sebichos (14)	127
Tarcus (18)	127

26TH DYNASTY – SAIS

Stephinates (7)	128
Nechepsos (6)	128
Nechao (8)	128
Psammetichus (54)	129
Nechao (6)	129
Psammuthis (6)	129
Uaphris (19)	130
Amosis (44)	130
Psammecherites (6 mths)	130

27TH DYNASTY – PERSIA

Cambyses (6)	131
Darius (36)	131
Xerxes (21)	131
Artabanus (7 mths)	132
Artaxerxes (41)	132
Xerxes (2 mths)	133
Sogdianus (7 mths)	133
Darius (19)	133

28TH DYNASTY – SAIS

Amyrteos (6)	133

29TH DYNASTY – MENDONIA

Nepherites (6)	134
Achoris (13)	134
Psammuthis (1)	134
Nepherites (4 mths)	134

30TH DYNASTY – SEBENNYTUS

Nectanebes (18)	135
Teos (2)	135
Nectanbus (18)	135

FIGURES IN BRACKETS = YEARS OF REIGN GIVEN BY MANETHO

4.01 REGISTER OF KINGS - MYTHICAL GOD-KINGS

Mythical God-kings

The classical historians relate the fabulous era of the Mythical God-kings and thus set the scene for the commencement of Egyptian history. In the "Ancient Chronical" the god reigns are disposed in lunar years as follows:-

The Sun reigned	33000	years
The Gods reigned	984	years
The Demi-Gods reigned	217	years
THE FABULOUS ERA	34201	years
The mortal kings	2324	years
EGYPT'S HISTORICAL SPAN	36525	years

Little is known of the fabulous period of God-kings of Egypt's distant antiquity, but the legends of them that have survived in the inscriptions are probably half-truths woven around factual events concerning mortal kings. These legends must represent the adaptation of ancient folklore at various stages of Egypt's pre-dynastic development. The conquests and defeats of invading tribes being remembered as monumental events. With the passing of time the chieftains or 'kings' involved became immortalised as gods in Egyptian antiquity. In an almost reverse manner, the old tribal gods became epitomised as Egyptian kings. The Kings' List of Manetho, and the Turin Canon both commenced with the reigns of gods and demi-gods.

Throughout most of Egyptian history the sun-god reigned supreme. Creator of all things, he is represented in various forms. In human form as ATUM wearing the double crown of Upper and Lower Egypt, as KHEPRA the beetle, creator god. As RE, RE-HERAKHTY, or HORUS, he is seen as a man with the head of a falcon, upon which is the sun-disk and a uraeus serpent. As Horus of Edfu, son of RE-HERAKHTY he is represented as a sun-disk with falcon wings and a uraeus on each side. He was combined with many other gods and as AMEN-RE he was the God of Thebes and later Egypt's national god as Thebes rose to power.

In the mythical legend of creation found with the cache of royal mummies at Deir el Bahri, the story relates how the almighty God Neberdjer (ATUM) begat himself in the form of KHEPRA and created all things out of nothingness, from the vast primeval waters. He then created the Gods SHU (Atmosphere) and TEFNUT (Moisture), who brought forth GEB (Earth) and NUT (Sky), who then brought forth OSIRIS, HORUS, SET, ISIS and NEPHTHYS, who then produced their offsprings - mankind.

In mythological terms the immediate descendants of these gods would be the pre-dynastic kings - the distant ancestors of the later dynastic kings the 'Sons of Re'.

The seeds of Egypt's mythology would thus find root in these pre-dynastic days. By the process of assimilation, fusion then separation into specific functionary gods, various deities emerged, each able to trace their descendancy from the original household and tribal gods and able to fit in nicely with the traditional folklore and creation myths.

The early religious beliefs of the common people thus form the base of what was to become Egypt's great pantheon - an hierarchical pyramid of over 2000 gods, with the almighty creator god at its peak. The following figures and cartouches represent some of the major gods.

SEKER
A Funerary God

KHEPER
God of Creation

AAH
Moon God

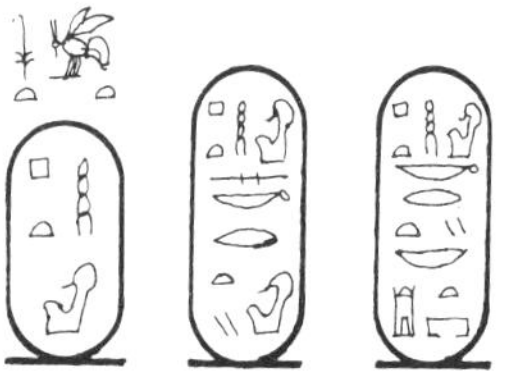

PTAH
Father of Gods

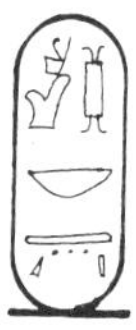

NEITH
Mother of Gods

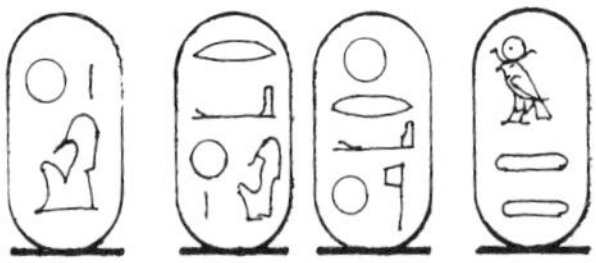

RE
The Sun-God

ATUM
Sun God

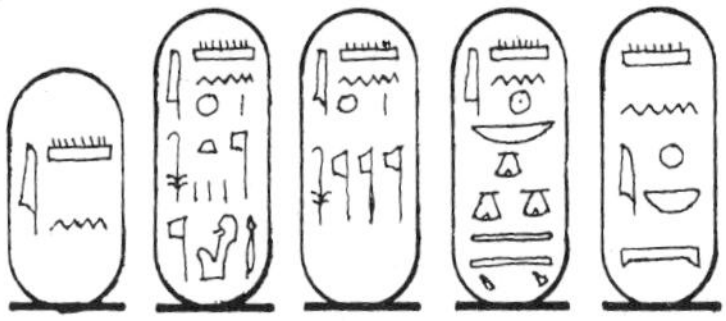

RE-HERAKHTY
Combined
RE & HORUS

AMEN/AMEN-RE
God of Thebes and all Egypt

MUT
Consort of Amen-Re

KHONS
Moon God

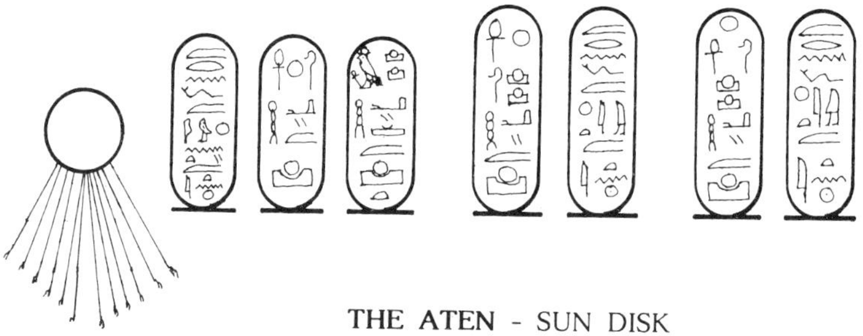

THE ATEN - SUN DISK
the god of Pharaoh Akhenaten

SHU
God of
atmosphere

TEFNUT
Goddess
of
moisture

GEB
The
Earth-God

NUT
Goddess
of
the sky

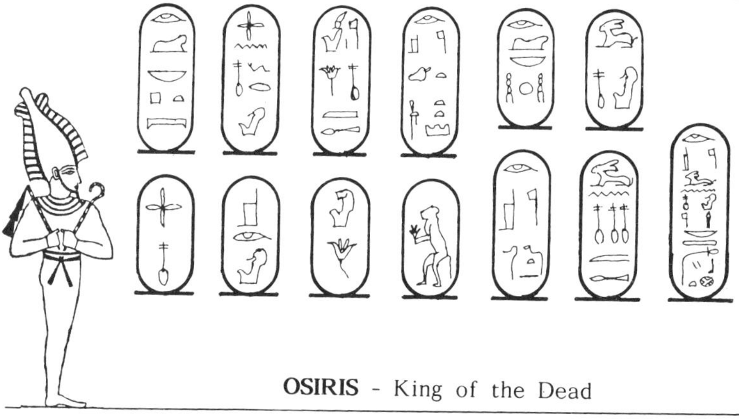

OSIRIS - King of the Dead

ISIS
Wife of Osiris

SET
God of Evil

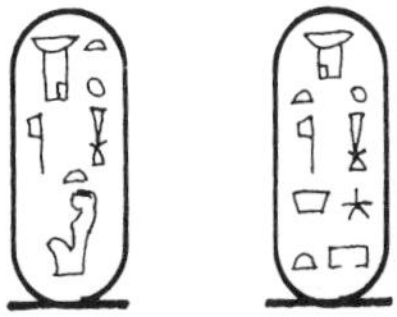

NEPHTHYS
Wife of Set

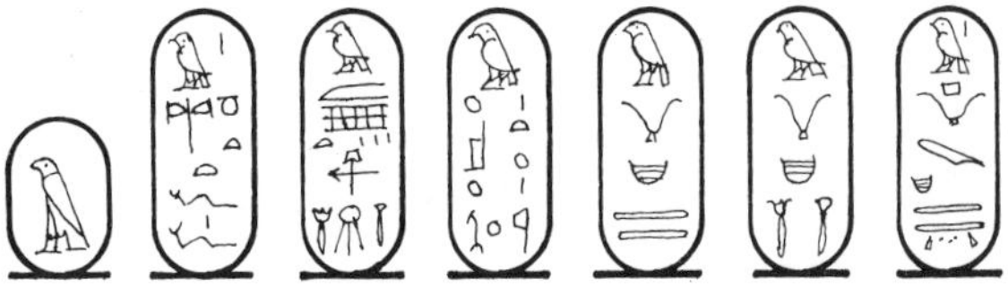

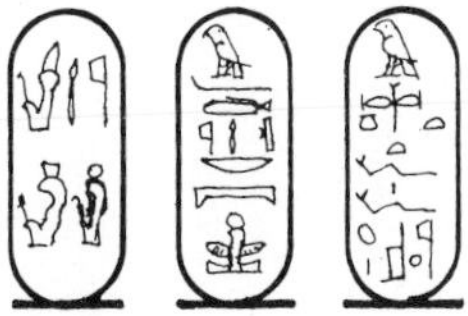

HORUS
The Falcon God

The **Winged Disk** - symbol of **HORUS OF EDFU**

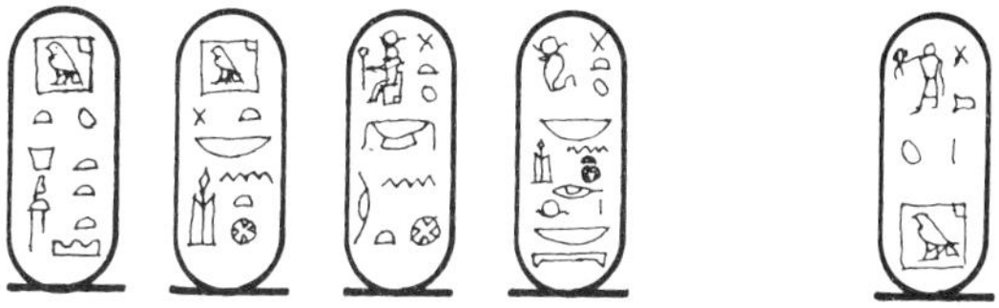

HATHOR
Sky Goddess

AHY
Son of Hathor

KHNUM - Creator God
of Mankind

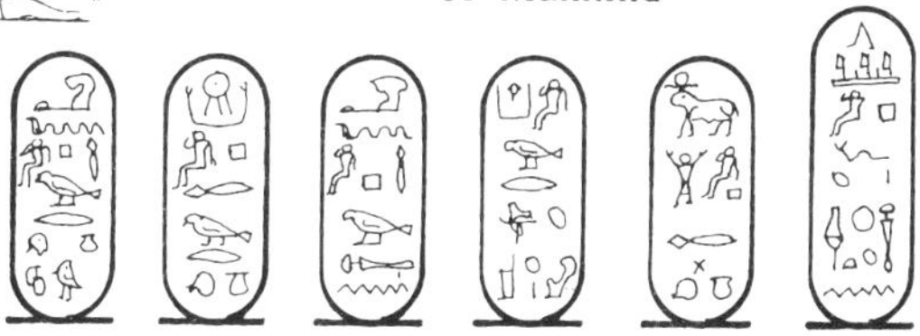

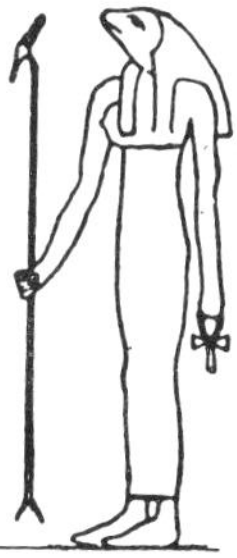

HEQET - Consort of KHNUM

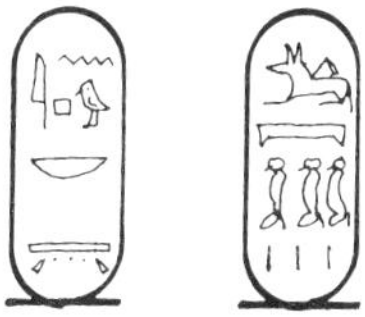

ANUBIS
Guardian of
the tomb

THOTH
Moon God of
wisdom & majic

MAAT
Goddess
of truth
& justice

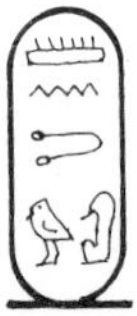

MONT
God of
Hermonthis

PAN
God of
the Delta

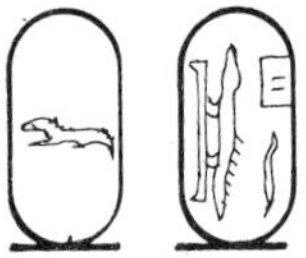

SOBEK
Son of Neith

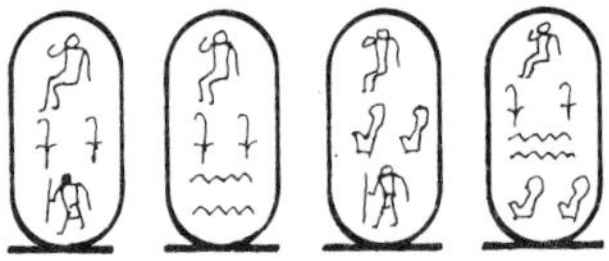

SENU

COLLECTIVE GODS

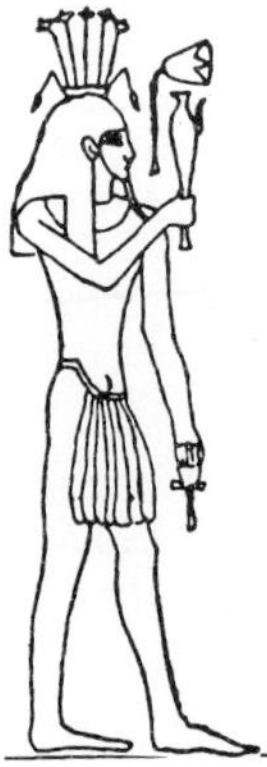

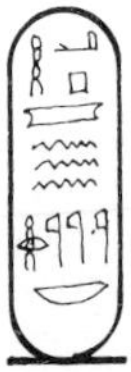

HAPY
God of
the Nile
&
all Gods

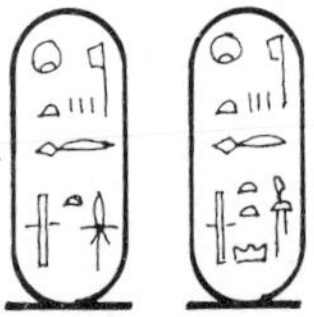

THE GREAT GODS
OF THE EAST
&
THE GREAT GODS
OF THE WEST

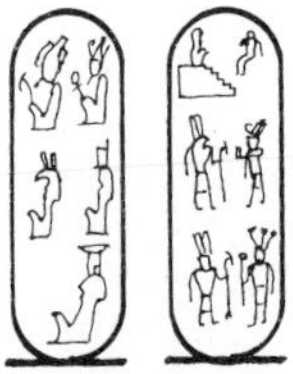

OSIRIS
HAROERIS
SET
ISIS
NEPHTHYS

4.02 REGISTER OF KINGS - PRE-DYNASTIC PERIOD

KINGS of LOWER EGYPT		KINGS of UPPER EGYPT	
Seka	25	De	25
Khaau	25	Re	25
Tau	25	Ka	25
Thesh	25	Sma	25
Neheb	25	Scorpion	26
Wadjin	25	Narmer	26
Menkhe	25	Aha	26

Two major sources of folklore helped fashion the mythology of ancient Egypt. One was the legend of creation, the other the legends woven around Horus, Set and Osiris.

Although the pantheon of gods appears mysterious and complicated, three elements of theology dictated the historical scene. These in the order of their appearance in Egypt were:- lunar worship, worship of the earth gods, and solar worship.

There is evidence that even before the onset of the dynastic period, a great civilisation flourished in Egypt. The nomadic tribes of the deserts of Upper Egypt had settled on the banks of the Nile, and the Delta land of Lower Egypt was peopled by the early invaders, the Mediterranean race of North Africa. These indigenous Egyptians probably worshipped the Moon as their creator god.

Ere many centuries had passed, the hunter gatherers of the Delta were absorbed by invading tribes from the East, who taught husbandry of the land after each inundation of the Nile. It was the time of the Earth Gods, Osiris had come to Egypt. Originally the God of vegetation, the Corn God, he embodied the attributes of the Moon God and later became the symbol of resurrection and thus the God of the Dead. The Delta prospered under the Osiris cult, Egypt was already divided into districts or nomes, and each nome had a king and he was the Osiris.

Another Earth God however, was to contest the Delta. From the East came the Semetic and mountain tribes of Syria and Arabia, bringing with them the worship of their God Setuth, eventually Egyptionised to Set. Vicious wars followed, and only the western delta Libians were able to check the onslaught of the followers of Set. These west delta Egyptians had their capital at Sais and worshipped the Goddess Neith. The reign of the Set tribes was a troublesome period for the worshippers of Neith, who could not accept their barbaric ways. It would seem likely that Set, having come down from Ombos (or driven down by Horus), conquered the Delta, but was then driven out by Horus.

Two Earth Gods arose in Lower Egypt. Concentrated around Memphis at the apex of the Nile Delta, were Seker and later Ptah (a Creator God), who became the chief deity of Memphis.

Meanwhile, in Upper Egypt a powerful race entered via the Red Sea and across the desert wadi routes, to settle at Edfu. These were the sun-worshippers of the Sky-God Horus, who may have originated in the highly civilised Indus Valley. They possessed metal weapons and brought in advanced culture and funerary beliefs. These followers of Horus were to become the Dynastic Race, which was to rule Egypt until its downfall at the hands of the Persians. Although some other sun-worshippers had previously entered the Delta, it was from Edfu that the Horus people swept down the Nile Valley, probably being halted at the Fayyum. The land of Egypt was divided into two separate kingdoms, with a king of Upper Egypt and a king of Lower Egypt. Both kings may have been followers of Horus, ruling different parts of Egypt. One king from Hieraconopolis in the South, and the other from Buto in the North.

The origin of these early pre-dynastic kings is not known for certain, but a legendary inscription from the Ptolemaic Temple of Edfu gives an account of what may be the arrival in Egypt of these noble people.

The inscription relates how the Sun-God Re-Herakhty, as an earthly king, came down (in the 363rd year of his reign), from the 'Land of the Bow' (Eastern Sudan, where the people fought with bows and arrows) and established himself and his followers at Edfu. The God's son Horus and his 'metal workers' armed with superior weapons, overcame the native flint-armed tribes at various places in Upper Egypt, then pursued the indigenous enemy into Lower Egypt, defeating the evil God Set and overcoming the Delta. Returning South he established the worship of Horus at Edfu and his father Re ordered that the symbol of Horus, a winged solar disk with a uraeus at each side, be set up in every sanctuary in Egypt. Horus had consolidated his power by claiming that his reign was supported by the goddesses of Upper and Lower Egypt, Nekhebet and Edjo. The symbol of Horus of Edfu can be seen over the entrance of many of the ancient temples of Egypt.

From the legend of Horus of Edfu we could summise that he was the leader of that noble breed of invaders who conquered the native Egyptians and imposed upon them the ruling class, later to be known as the dynastic race.

The later dynastic kings embodied the titles Horus, Nekhebet, and Edjo, Re (Son of Re), and King of the North and South in their titulary. The title 'Son of Re', although appearing for the first time later in the dynastic period, suggests direct descent from the Sun-God Re. Actual sun worship probably began under the northern followers of Horus and there is evidence that in the early struggles, the North was in fact victorious over the South.

The final unification process undoubtedly began with the conquest of the North by the South, under the Kings Scorpion, Aha and Narmer, but whether any of these was Manetho's legendary King Menes is not known. Perhaps unification was not confirmed until Menes, or perhaps Menes represented an amalgam of these early kings.

The pre-dynastic kings listed on the Palermo Stone have not been discovered, but their hieroglyphic names are shown below.

KINGS of LOWER EGYPT

Seka 

Khaau 

Tau 

Thesh 

Neheb 

Wadjin 

Menkhe 

KINGS of UPPER EGYPT

The following names have also been discovered:-

De 

Re 

Ka 

Sma 

SCORPION c 3000 BC

King Scorpion

King Scorpion seems to have been involved in the early struggles for unification of the two lands. Two mace heads from Hieraconopolis the ancient capital of Upper Egypt, show scenes representing victory, reorganisation and peace. In one scene he wears the white crown of Upper Egypt and performs an agricultural rite. In another he wears the red crown of Lower Egypt and sits before Horus and the defeated enemy.

HIERACONOPOLIS

AHA c 3000 BC

The Horus King Aha

King Aha is possibly the Menes of Manetho's list, founder of the 1st Dynasty. A tablet from the tomb of his Queen Neithhotep (a northern princess) contains both his 'Horus' name Aha as King of Upper and Lower Egypt and a 'Two Ladies' name Men. The scene represents "receiving the South and the North". Tombs at Abydos (Amelineau, Petrie), and Saqqara (Emery).

THINIS

NARMER c 3000 BC

The Horus King Narmer

This king is considered by some to be the Menes of Manetho's list in preference to King Aha. He is depicted on the famous Narmer Pallet wearing the crown of both Upper and Lower Egypt. The scenes represent a victory for the South over the North, and unification of the two lands. His name was also found on items in the tomb of Queen Neithhotep at Naqada. Tomb at Abydos (Amelineau, Petrie).

THINIS

4.03 REGISTER OF KINGS - EARLY DYNASTIC PERIOD

c 2935-2592 BC

1ST DYNASTY c 2935-2785 BC (THINIS)

2935	Menes	Horus Aha	29
	Teti	Horus Narmer	29
	Iti	Horus Djer (Zer)	29
	Ita	Horus Uadji (Zet)	30
	Zemti	Horus Udimu (Den)	30
	Merpaba	Horus Anedjib (Enezib)	30
	Semsem	Horus Semerkhet	31
	Kebh	Horus Qaa (Ka'a)	31
2785	Bauneter	Horus Qaa (Ka'a)	31

2ND DYNASTY c 2785-2665 BC (THINIS)

2785	Bedjau	Horus Hotepsekhemui	32
	Kakau	Horus Reneb	32
	Baneteren	Horus Neteren	33
	Wadjnes	Horus Sekhemib-Perenmaat	33
	Peribsen	Set Peribsen	33
	Sendi		34
	Kare (Aa ka)		34
	Neferkare		34
	Neferkaseker	Horus Khasekhem	35
	Hudjefa	Horus Khasekhem	35
2665	Beby (Djadjay)	Horus Khasekhemui-Nebuihopinef	35

3RD DYNASTY c 2665-2592 BC (MEMPHIS)

2665	Nebka	Horus Zanakhte	36
2647	Djoser	Horus Neterkhet	36
	Djoser Teti		37
	Sedjes (Ahtes)		37
2628		Horus Sekhemkhet	37
2622		Horus Kha Ba	37
2616	Huni (Neferkare)		38
	Nebkare		38
	Shairu	Horus Shairu	38

The first dynasty began with King Menes and according to Manetho, came from Thinis. Menes is said to have founded Memphis and built a temple to Ptah. This probably represents an effort by him to consolidate the kingdom by establishing the seat of government there. Memphis probably existed before Menes became king but was thus raised in importance by him because of its strategic location both for commerce and as a centre of the community.

The catalyst for the development of the religion with its multifarious deities and cult legends, was the in-built stubbornness of the common Egyptian people, who persisted in their local beliefs and ancient folklore. The astute priests who themselves were part of the ruling class, countered this by stressing the flexibility of the religious system. Absorbing and emphasising the local beliefs as necessary to accommodate every class of society.

Over the first three dynasties however, the struggle for supremacy continued. Religion still divided the two Egypts. The king had for long been regarded as the living incarnation of the ruling deity. The fusion of Osiris, Seker and Ptah probably served to satisfy the delta people and the king was using the title Horus as his main name, so the sun-worshippers of the South would still feel secure, but they would be seeking more recognition: after all they were the ruling class.

Throughout Egyptian history the names of the kings reveal their religious affiliations. Apart from the established titles or prefixes discussed under Kings and Cartouches, page 9, the cartouche names themselves tell us the cult currently in favour at the time of the king's coronation (his prenomen), and the family cult or cult in favour at the time of the king's birth (his nomen or Son of Re name).

The names of the early dynastic kings betray to us the power struggle between the North and the South, and reveal the bitter conflict between the religions of Set and Horus.

It is not clear why a change of dynasty should have been indicated for the 2nd Thinite line. Perhaps it was because unification was once again achieved after a troublesome period following the death of the 1st Dynasty King Ka'a. King Wadjnes of the 2nd Dynasty changed his allegiance from the God Horus to the God Set.

The 3rd Dynasty however, saw a line of rulers from Memphis gaining the kingship, thus the southern rulers lost control of Egypt to the northern rulers. An indication of the conflict which was to be the pattern for kingship for the remainder of the dynastic era.

MENES 1st Dynasty c 2935 BC

Men

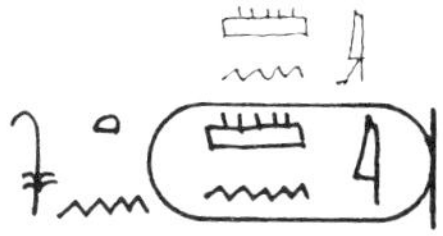

Meni

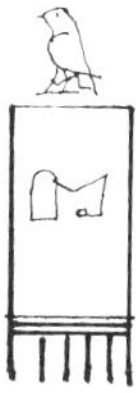

MENES - legendary founder of the 1st Dynasty, the king who united Upper and Lower Egypt. He diverted the Nile to found Memphis and protect it from flooding. He was killed by a hippopotamus after reigning 62 years, M. For comments on Aha see also page 26. Aha's tombs are at Abydos (Petrie), Saqqara (Emery).

Aha

THINIS

TETI 1st Dynasty

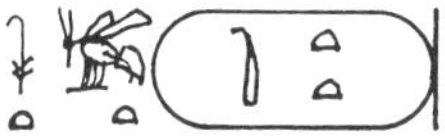

37
46

Teti

37

Teti

ATHOTHIS - son of Menes he reigned 57 years and built a royal palace at Memphis. He was a physician and wrote books on anatomy which were still extant in Manetho's days, M. Little else is known of Athothis, but for comments on Narmer see page 26.
Narmer's tomb found at Abydos (Petrie).

Narmer

THINIS

ITI 1st Dynasty

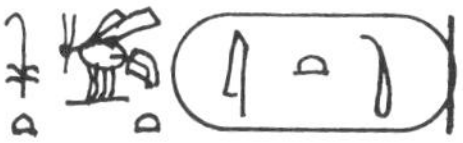

Iti

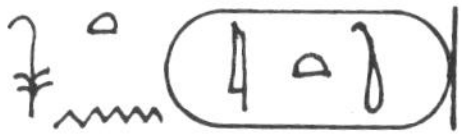

30
46

Iti

ATETH. **KENKENES** - son of Teti, reigned 31 years, M. Iti is 3rd on the Abydos List and is thus equated with Manetho's Kenkenes. Iti follows Zer on jar sealings from Zer's tomb at Abydos. A mummy's arm with fine jewels was also found and the tomb had 317 sacrificial? burials.
Tombs-Abydos (Petrie), Saqqara (Emery), Saqqara (Quibell)

Djer (Zer)

THINIS

ITA 1st Dynasty

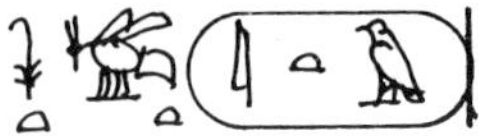

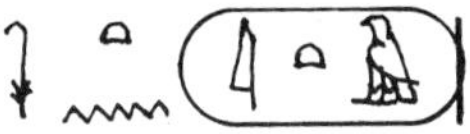

29
46

Ita

Ata

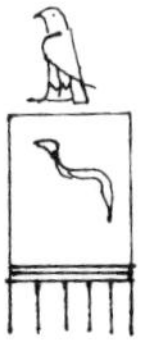

UENEPHES - reigned 23 years, built pyramids at Cochone (Saqqara). In his time a great plague raged through Egypt, M. Uadji's tombs had many sacrificial? burials. In his Abydos tomb were 300 model bulls heads. His comb bears the winged disk symbol bearing Horus in his barque. Tombs-Abydos (Petrie), Giza (Petrie).

Uadji (Zet) THINIS

ZEMTI 1st Dynasty

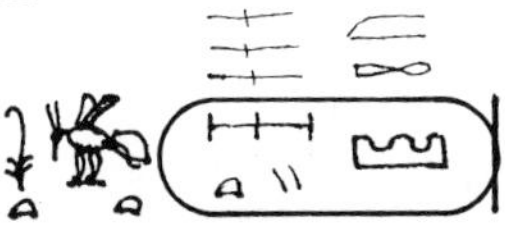

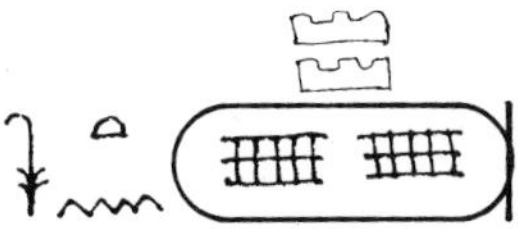

Zemti

Semti

USAPHAIDOS - son of Uenephes, reigned 20 years, M. An ebony tablet from Abydos bears the names Zemti and Den and the king wearing the crown of Upper and Lower Egypt dances before a seated figure, possibly the god Osiris. Festival of the followers of Horus in his reign. Tombs-Abydos (Petrie), Saqqara (Emery).

Udimu (Den) THINIS

MERPABA 1st Dynasty

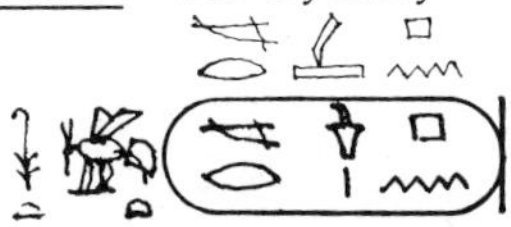

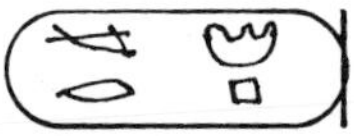

Mer pa ba

Mer pa ba

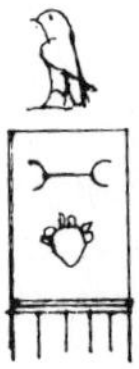

MIEBIDOS - reigned 26 years, M. The first king of the Saqqara List, thus perhaps the first Thinite king to gain the full support of the northern people. On some objects his name was usurped by the next southern King Semerkhet, who was then omitted by the Saqqara List. Tombs-Abydos (Petrie), Saqqara (Quibell).

Anedjib (Enezib) THINIS

SEMSEM 1st Dynasty

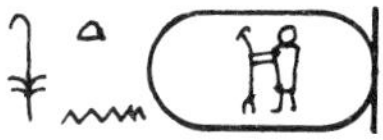

Sem sem (Nekht) Sem em Ptah (Hu)

SEMEMPSES - son of Miebidos, reigned 18 years. In his time a terrible pestilence afflicted Egypt, M. He may have usurped the throne from King Miebidos and his reign was recorded on the Palermo Stone as "of great calamities". The bones of a dwarf were found in his tomb at Abydos (Petrie).

Semerkhet THINIS

KEBH 1st Dynasty

Kebh Qebh

This king appears on the Abydos, Saqqara and Turin Lists, following Semsem on two of them. For this reason he has been identified by some with Bieneches of Manetho, who is shown as the last king of Dynasty 1, see Bauneter below. The Horus King Qaa could be identified with either of them.

Qaa (Ka'a) THINIS

BAUNETER 1st Dynasty c 2785 BC

Bau neter Biu nutje

BIENECHES - son of Semempses, reigned 26 years. Last king of the 1st Dynasty, M. Qaa's elaborate tomb at Saqqara did not have sacrificial? burials, but his Abydos tomb had 26. The dynasty ends but the reason for its downfall was not recorded. Tombs-Abydos (Petrie), Saqqara (Emery).

Qaa (Ka'a) THINIS

NEITHHOTEP Q 1st Dynasty c 2935 BC

This queen's tomb was found at Naqada (de Morgan). In it as well as her own inscriptions, were found the names of her husband Aha and of the Horus King Narmer. Her name incorporates the Goddess Neith of Sais and thus suggests that she was a northern princess. Perhaps her marriage was used to pacify the North after unification.

MERNEITH Q 1st Dynasty

Her great tomb at Abydos with its sacrificial? burials (Petrie), suggests that she was important, perhaps a sovereign ruler in her own right. The Horus name Djer was found on items from her other tomb at Saqqara (Emery), so perhaps she was Djer's consort. Her name suggests that she was another northern princess.

BEDJAU 2nd Dynasty c 2785 BC

Be djau

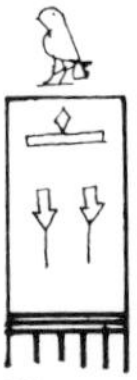

BOETHOS - reigned 28 years and during his reign many people perished in a chasm of the earth which opened up near Bubastis, M. Little else is known of this king but his Horus name Hotepsekhemui means 'the two powers are pacified', suggesting revival from a disturbed period to the founding of the new dynasty.

Hotepsekhemui

THINIS

KAKAU 2nd Dynasty

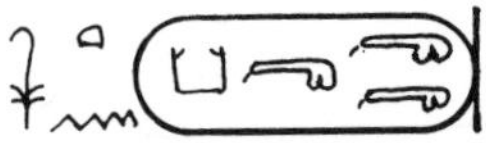

Ka kau

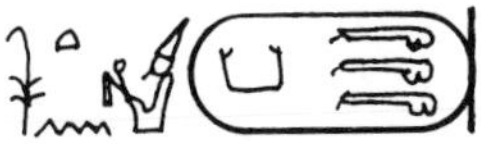

Ka kau

KAIECHOS - 'The Bull of Bulls', reigned 39 years, under him various animals were appointed to be gods. Bulls at Memphis, Mnevis at Heliopolis, and the Ram at Mendes, M. His name is found on a granite statue from Memphis, with names of his predecessor Hotepsekhemui and his successor Neteren.

Reneb

THINIS

BANETEREN 2nd Dynasty

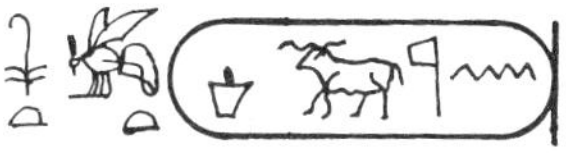

Ba neter n

Ba neter u

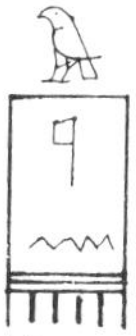

BINOTHRIS - reigned 47 years and in his time it was decreed that women might hold office of the imperial government, M. He had no sons so he tried to arrange for his daughter to succeed him, but no evidence to show that this occurred. Indications of civil war with reference to the destruction of the 'House of the North'.

Neteren

THINIS

WADJNES 2nd Dynasty

Wadj nes

Wadj nes

TLAS - reigned 17 years, M. Probably the Horus Sekhemib, whose tomb was found at Abydos (Petrie). There was political and religious revelations in his reign and he changed his Horus name to Set Peribsen. There is evidence that the tombs of the previous kings had been ritually burned at this restoration of Set.

Sekhemib-Perenmaat

THINIS

PERIBSEN 2nd Dynasty

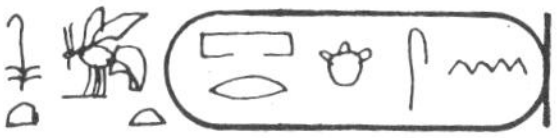

Per ib sen

Per ib s

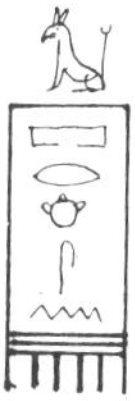

This is King Wadjnes after he changed his affiliation from Horus to Set. The reason for this change is not clear, but it was no doubt connected with the ethnic power struggle between the two religious groups. King Peribsen obviously rejected the religion of Horus or at least he attempted to introduce Set into the royal titles.

Peribsen

THINIS

SENDI 2nd Dynasty

Sendi

Sendi

SETHENES - reigned 41 years, M. He revised a medical papyrus from the 1st Dynasty of King Zemti. He must have been a powerful king, for his cult survived until much later. A stele from the tomb of a priest in the 4th Dynasty bears Sendi's cartouche and there is evidence that he was still revered in the 26th Dynasty.

THINIS

KARE 2nd Dynasty

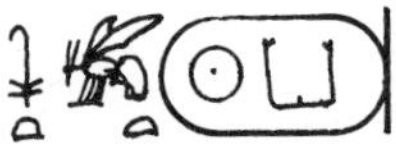

Ka Re

Aa ka (Neter ka)

CHAIRES - reigned 17 years, M. His name was found on a green steatite cylinder seal and he is listed on the Turin Canon, otherwise little known of him. This may have been the first appearance of the symbol of the Sun-God Re in a cartouche, suggesting that he was conencted with the emergence of the cult, but see Neferkare below.

THINIS

NEFERKARE 2nd Dynasty

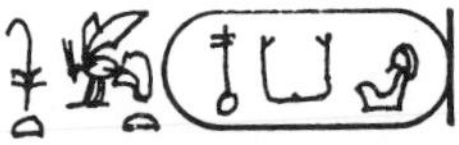

Nefer ka Re

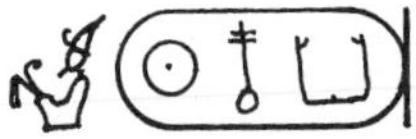

38
47

Nefer ka Re

NEPHERCHERES - reigned 25 years and during his time the Nile flooded with honey for 11 days, M. His name is from the Saqqara List only, but incorporates the Sun-God Re in a cartouche, perhaps confirming the rise to power of this God's cult. Some authorities believe that this was too early for the emergence of the Re cult.

THINIS

NEFERKASEKER 2nd Dynasty

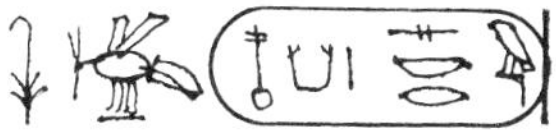

Nefer ka seker

Nefer ka seker

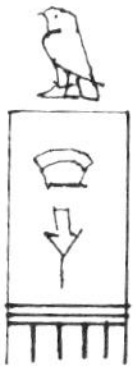

SESOCHRIS - reigned 48 years, his height was 5 cubits (about 8ft), M. Statues and other items were found at Hieraconopolis showing him wearing the crown of Upper Egypt. An inscription on a stone vase suggests that he re-united Egypt after the religious wars of Horus and Seth. His name means 'rising of the power'.

Khasekhem

THINIS

HUDJEFA 2nd Dynasty

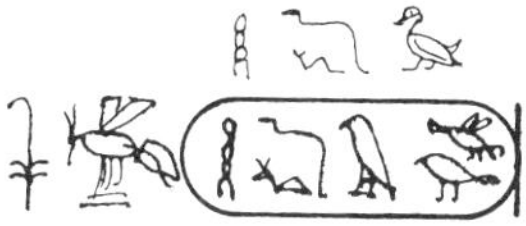

Hu djefa

Hu djefa

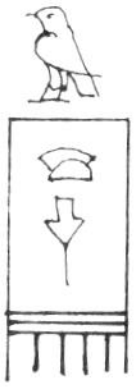

Name from the Turin Canon and Saqqara List but not found on monuments. He is thought to be identified with Neferkaseker above, ie. the Horus Kha Sekhem, in whose reign long civil wars are recorded. The Horus and Set wars seemed to have been resolved, but it must have been an uneasy peace, (see the next king).

Khasekhem

THINIS

BEBY (DJADJAY) 2nd Dynasty

c 2665 BC

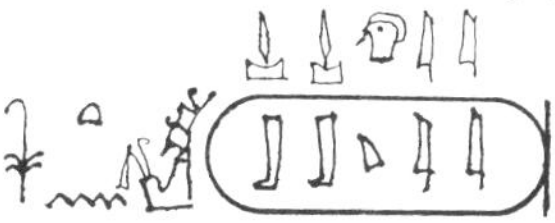

Bebi

Beby (Djadjay)

CHENERES - reigned 30 years, M. His name means 'the rising of the two powers, the two powers are at peace'. Which suggests final consolidation of the North and the South in a united Egypt. Remains of his temple at Hieraconopolis. His golden sceptre was found in his tomb at Abydos (Petrie).

Khasekhemui-Nebuihopinef

THINIS

NEBKA 3rd Dynasty 2665-2647 BC

Neb ka

Neb ka

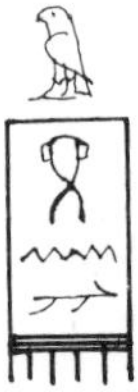

Zanakhte

NECHEROPHES - reigned 28 years and in his time during a battle against the Libians, the moon so increased its size that the Libians submitted in fear, M. The face of Zanakhte can be seen on a sculptured talet (Wadi Maghara). His reign was the start of a new Memphite dynasty. Cenotaph at Beit Khallaf (Garstang).

MEMPHIS

DJOSER 3rd Dynasty 2647-2628 BC

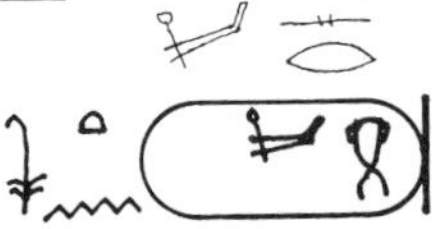

37

Djoser

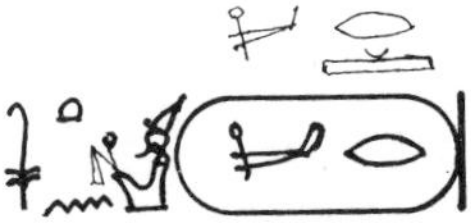

Djoser

Neterkhet

ZOSSER. **TOSORTHROS** - reigned 29 years and built a house of stone. Because of his medical knowledge he was called Aselphius the medical king, M. Manetho may have been referring to Imhotep his great architect, the designer of Djoser's step pyramid at Saqqara. Djoser's tomb was at Beit Khallaf near Abydos (Garstang).

MEMPHIS

TYREIS, MESOCHRIS, SOYPHIS 3rd Dynasty

Next followed 3 kings from Memphis. According to Manetho they were as follows:-

TYREIS - reigned 7 years.

MESOCHRIS - reigned 17 years.

SOYPHIS - reigned 16 years.

Nothing has been found of these kings.

MEMPHIS

DJOSER TETI 3rd Dynasty

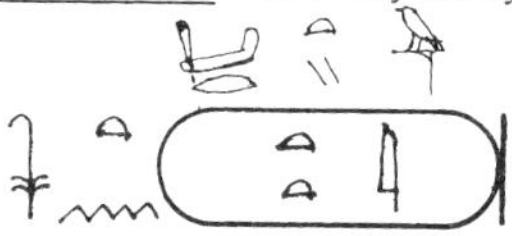

36

Djoser Teti — Djoser Teti

TOSERTASIS - reigned 19 years, M. Nothing is known of this king other than his cartouche recorded on the Saqqara and Turin Lists, and possibly as Teti in the Abydos List. Identified with the above Manetho king only by similarity of names. The Turin List gives him 6 years, so perhaps he is Tyreis of Manetho.

MEMPHIS

SEDJES (AHTES) 3rd Dynasty

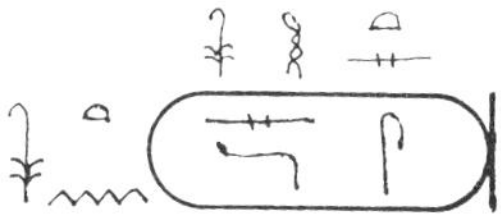

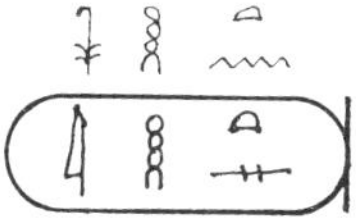

Sedjes — Ahtes

ACHES - reigned 42 years, M. Identified with Manetho's king only by similarity of names. His cartouches are found on the Palermo Stone, and the Abydos List after Teti. Otherwise nothing known of him despite Manetho's claim for a long reign. He may be however, the Horus King Sekhemkhet, see below.

MEMPHIS

HORUS **SEKHEMKHET** 3rd Dynasty 2628-2622 BC

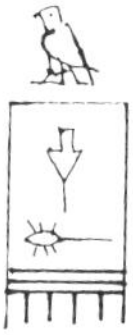

This king had a pyramid at Saqqara, "The Unfinished Pyramid", in which was found an alabaster sarcophagus still sealed, but upon opening, it was found to be empty. He may possibly be the above King Sedjes.

MEMPHIS

HORUS **KHA BA** 3rd Dynasty 2622-2616 BC

This king has not been positively identified with any Manetho or Kings List name. A pyramid "The Layer Pyramid" at Zawyet el-Aryan near Giza (Barstanti) is thought to have been his.

MEMPHIS

HUNI (NEFERKARE) 3rd Dynasty 2616-2592 BC

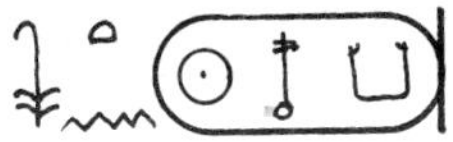

34
47

Nefer ka Re Huni

KERPHERES, M. He is known from the cartouches of the Saqqara and Turin Lists. His daughter probably became the wife of the next King Sneferu, since she bore the title 'Daughter of the God'. The pyramid at Maidum allotted to Sneferu, may have been started by him. The last king of the dynasty, but see Shairu below.

MEMPHIS

NEBKARE 3rd Dynasty

Neb ka Re

This king found on the Saqqara List, following Djoser Teti, has not been identified elsewhere. Some have equated him with King Sedjes but he may possibly be equated with King Nebka the founder of the Dynasty.

MEMPHIS

SHAIRU 3rd Dynasty

Shairu

Shairu

This king, whose name was found in a rock inscription at El-Kab, remains an enigma. This seemingly ephemeral ruler is identified by some with Manetho's **SEPHURIS** and by others with Manetho's **SORIS**, the founder of the 9th Dynasty. He probably represents the transition between the two dynasties.

MEMPHIS

4.04 REGISTER OF KINGS - OLD KINGDOM
c 2592-2160 BC

4TH DYNASTY 2592-2477 BC (MEMPHIS)

2592	Seneferu	(Snofru)	41
2568	Khufu	(Cheops)	41
2545	Radjedef		41
2537	Rakhaef	(Chephren)	42
2511	Menkaure	(Mycerinus)	42
2483	Shepseskaf		42

5TH DYNASTY 2477-2329 BC (ELEPHANTINE)

2477	Userkaf		43
2470	Sahure		43
2456	Kakai	Nefererkare	43
2446	Shepseskare	Ini	44
2439	Khaneferre	Reneferf	44
2432	Ini	Niuserre	44
2405	Menkauhor		45
2397	Isesi	Djedkare	45
2358	Unis	Sa Unis	46

6TH DYNASTY 2328-2160 BC (MEMPHIS)

2328	Teti	Sa Teti	46
2296	Userkare	Ity	46
2295	Pepi I	Meryre	47
2261	Merenre I	Antyemsaf	47
2256	Pepi II	Neferkare	47
2162	Merenre II	Antyemsaf	48
2161	Nitocris Q	Netiqerty	48
	Imhotep		48

The 4th Dynasty continued under Memphite rule and the kings built great pyramids. Still the struggle of kingship prevailed, but now within the royal family itself. The dynasty had been founded by the marriage of Snofru to the daughter of Neferkare, the last king of the 3rd Dynasty. Three sons of Khufu vied for the throne and each ruled in their turn. The worship of the Sun-God Re began to gain prominence during this period, and the title 'Son of Re' was first used by Radjedef to set a practice which was to last throughout Egypt's history.

Re's rise to almighty power began in the 4th Dynasty and was the downfall of the Khufu family. Elements of Re had begun to appear in the names of his immediate descendants Radjedef and Khafre, and the 5th Dynasty was ushered in by a new family arising from the High Priest of Re. The legend from the Westcar Papyrus prophosises that the first three kings of the 5th Dynasty were to be conceived by devine birth through the wife of the High Priest of Re, Reddjedet. Although the legend was probably invented at a later date, it reflects the mythology created to cover the seizure of the throne by the followers of the Sun-God Re.

Although the power of the cult of Re would ebb and flow over the remainder of Egypt's history, the triumph of Re was secured. From then on all genuine kings of Egypt used the title 'Son of Re' before their family name.

The old dogmas of the tribal gods were not abandoned however, the mythology was simply modified to suit each locality. From the fusion of two tribal gods emerged three, the new god with the attributes of the existing two and the two still being retained somewhere in the pantheon.

Manetho's 5th Dynasty was from Elephantine, but the capital was still at Memphis. The early kings of the period built sun temples and large mastaba tombs and the pyramids decreased in size. In the 6th Dynasty the kingship again fell to the Memphites.

Egypt had now become politically unstable, nobles had grown powerful and the kingship was threatened. Teti a non-royal, came to the throne to start the 6th Dynasty. He too was a sun-worshipper. It was during this dynasty that the great Pepy II reigned for about 90 years, but this in itself may have started the downfall of the dynasty. In his old age a weakening rule may have served to further increase the unrest amongst the nobles.

Pepy's son Merenre ruled for a short while. His sister Nitocris followed him to the throne but the true power of the kingship was lost and the 6th Dynasty ended with the first female Pharaoh.

SENEFERU 4th Dynasty 2592-2568 BC

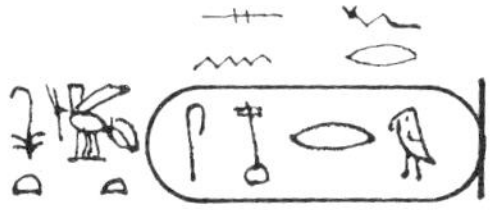 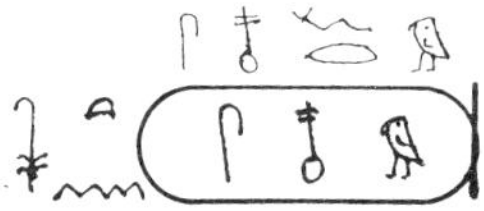

Se neferu Se neferu

SNOFRU. **SORIS,** M. Founder of the dynasty. He had two pyramids at Dahshur, "The Shining Pyramid" or "The Red Pyramid" and "The Southern Shining Pyramid" or "The Bent Pyramid". A third pyramid at Maidum may be his. Name found on a relief in Wadi Maghara. He built many ships and had campaigns in Nubia.

Nebmaat MEMPHIS

KHUFU 4th Dynasty 2568-2545 BC

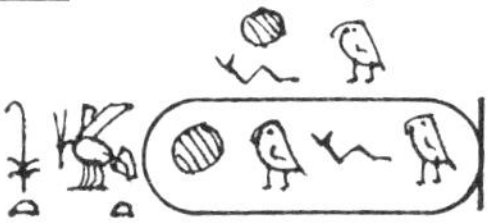 

Khu fu Khu fu

CHEOPS. **SUPHIS,** he wrote The Sacred Book, M. Son of Snofru. Pyramid at Giza, "The Pyramid which is the Place of Sunrise and Sunset" or "The Great Pyramid of Giza". Empty sarcophagus found in pyramid. The pyramid is alligned to the four cardinal points. His name is derived from the god of creation Khnum.

Medjdu MEMPHIS

RADJEDEF 4th Dynasty 2545-2537 BC

 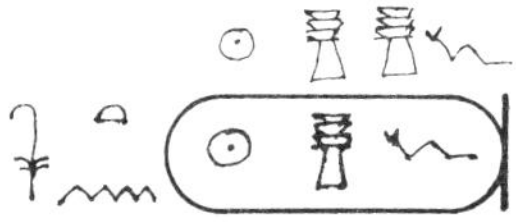

Ra djed f (Djed f Re) Ra djed f

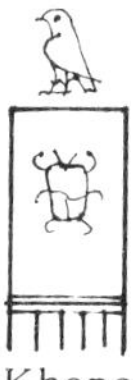

RATOISES, M. Son of Khufu. Pyramid at Abu Rawash, "The Pyramid which is the Sky". His father and his brother are mentioned in the Westcar Papyrus of magicians' tales. The symbol of the Sun-god Re is incorporated in his name. The name could be translated as 'Re is his strength'.

Kheper MEMPHIS

RAKHAEF 4th Dynasty 2537-2511 BC

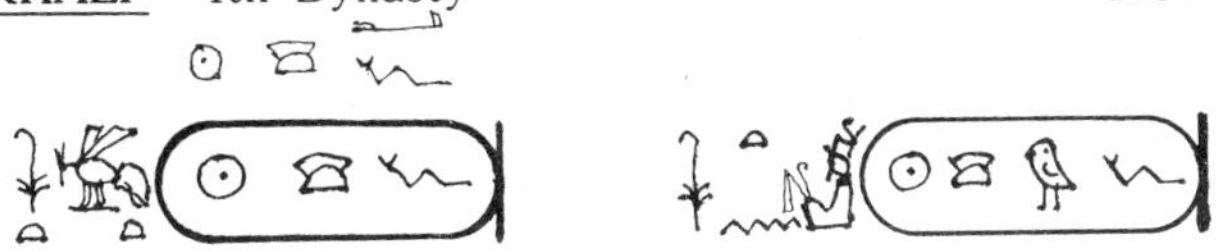

Ra kha f Kha f Re

CHEPHREN. **SUPHIS,** M. Brother of Khufu. He built a pyramid at Giza, "The Great Pyramid" or "The Second Pyramid of Giza". Empty sarcophagus found in pyramid. He promoted the worship of Isis and his wife Merisankh restored the worship of Thoth.

Userib MEMPHIS

MENKAURE 4th Dynasty 2511-2483 BC

48
51

Men kau Re Men kau Re

MYCERINUS. **MENCHERES,** M. Son of Khufu. He built a pyramid at Giza, "The Divine Pyramid" or "The Third Pyramid at Giza". Empty sarcophagus found in pyramid but a mummy found in a wooden coffin in the pyramid may be his.

Kakhet MEMPHIS

SHEPSESKAF 4th Dynasty 2483-2479 BC

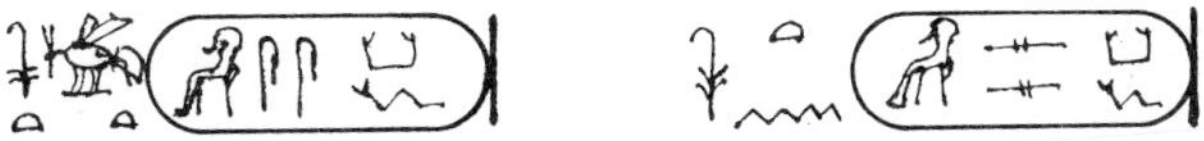

Shepses ka f Shepses ka f

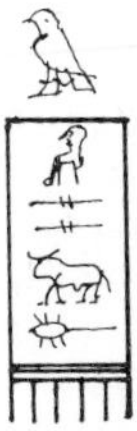

BICHERIS, M. Identified by some with Manetho's **SEBERCHERES.** He is said to have invented geometry and astronomy. Pyramid at Saqqara, "The Purified Pyramid", a sarcophagus-shaped structure. His eldest daughter Maatkha married Ptah-Shepses who was head prophet of The Priesthood of Ptah of Memphis.

Shepseskhet MEMPHIS

USERKAF 5th Dynasty 2477-2470 BC

User ka f

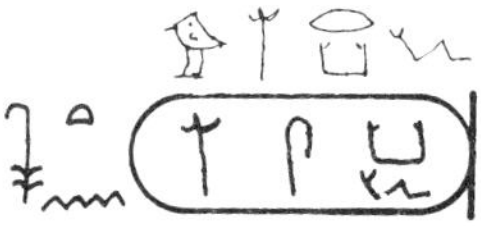

User ka f

Irmaat

USERCHERES, M. High Priest of the God Re of Annu (Heliopolis). He seized the throne to found the dynasty. During his reign worship of the Sun-God Re increased. Pyramid at Saqqara, "The Pyramid which is Pure of Places". Manetho gave the dynasty as from Elephantine, but all evidence is that it came from Heliopolis.

ELEPHANTINE

SAHURE 5th Dynasty 2470-2456 BC

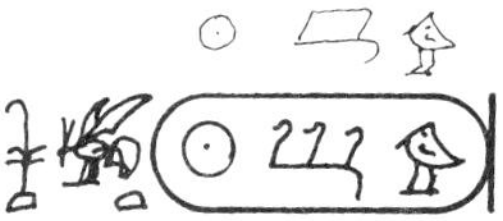

Sahu Re

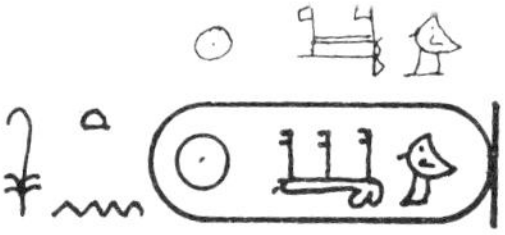

Sahu Re

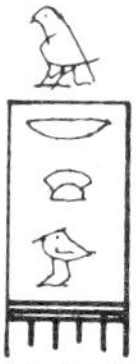

Nebkhau

SEPHRES, M. He is shown on a relief at Wadi Maghara. He made an expedition to the land of Punt to get incense and precious woods. Pyramid at Abusir, "The Pyramid of the Shining Spirit". He is one of three brothers named in a legend on the Westcar Papyrus, prophesised to be born of the Sun-God Re.

ELEPHANTINE

KAKAI 5th Dynasty 2456-2446 BC

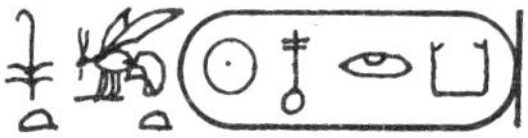

Nefer er ka Re

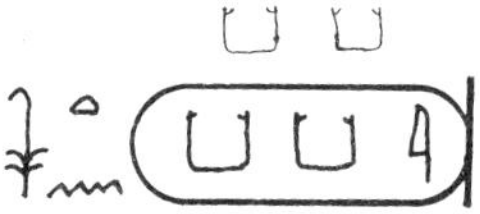

Ka kai

Userkhau

NEPHERCHERES, M. The third brother mentioned on the Westcar Papyrus, wife of User-Re. Conceived by Reddjedet through the God Re and destined to succeed to the throne and start the new dynasty. Userkaf, Sahure and Kakai. Pyramid at Abusir, "The Pyramid of the Ba-spirit".

ELEPHANTINE

SHEPSESKARE 5th Dynasty 2446-2439 BC

73

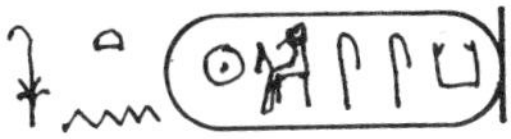

Ini Shepses ka Re

SISIRES - reigned 7 years, M. Little known of him, but his name appears on the Saqqara Kings List, and on the Turin Canon, where he is given a reign of 7 years.

ELEPHANTINE

KHANEFERRE 5th Dynasty 2439-2432 BC

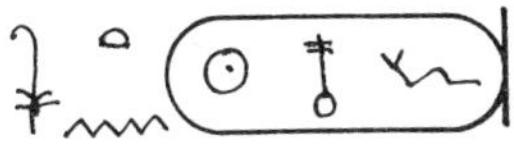

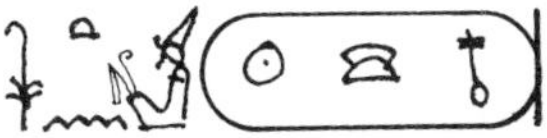

Re nefer f Kha nefer Re

CHERES, M. Pyramid at Abusir, "The Pyramid which is Divine of the Ba-spirits". Shown on the Turin Canon and the Saqqara List as Khaneferre and on the Abydos List as Raneferef. Nothing much known of this king but the foundations of a pyramid at Abusir, "The Pyamid which is Divine of Ba-spirits", probably belong to him.

Neferkhau

ELEPHANTINE

INI 5th Dynasty 2432-2401 BC

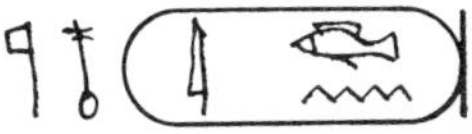
73

Ni user Re Ini

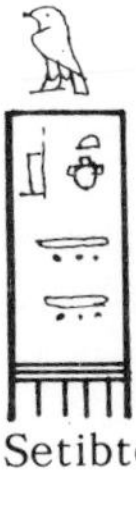

RATHURES, M. Held war campaigns in Sinai, and recorded his name at Wadi Maghara. Pyramid at Abusir, "The Pyramid which is Estbalished of Places". Sun temple near Abu Ghurab with boat-pit. Oblisk replaces pyramid as emblem of Re. Son of Re name officially established. Each king now has two cartouche names.

Setibtowe

ELEPHANTINE

MENKAUHOR 5th Dynasty 2405-2397 BC

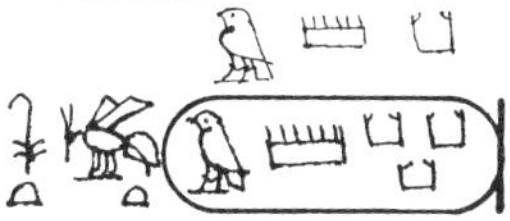

Men kau Hor

Men kau Hor

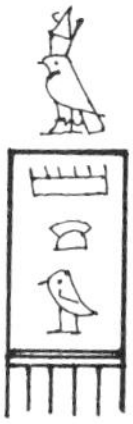

Menkhau

MENCHERES - reigned 9 years, M. Name on the Turin, Abydos and Saqqara Lists. His relief and name also found in the bull-pits at Saqqara and inscriptions at Wadi Maghara. He built a pyramid, "The Pyramid which is Holy of Places". This pyramid has not yet been discovered, but it should be at Saqqara.

ELEPHANTINE

ISESI 5th Dynasty 2397-2358 BC

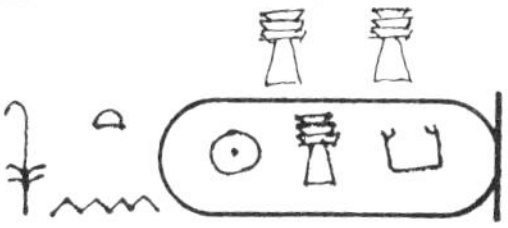

Djed ka Re

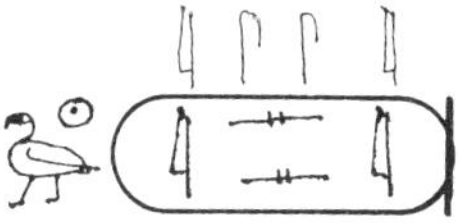

Isesi

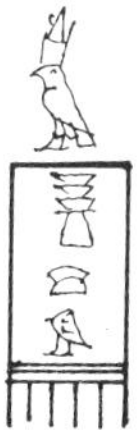

Djedkhau

TANCHERES, M. Name at Wadi Maghara and Wadi Hammamat. Pyramid at Saqqara, "The Beautiful Pyramid". His name was also found on a papyrus from Saqqara. The Prisse Papyrus which contains "The Precepts of Ptah-Hotep", a beautiful narrative on moral principles, is also dated from his reign.

ELEPHANTINE

ISESI 5th Dynasty 2397-2358 BC

Isesi

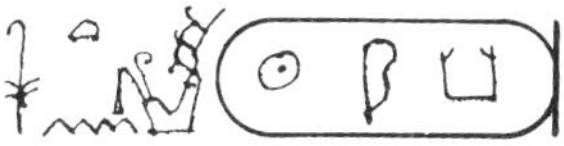

91
122

Maat ka Re

Djedkhau

These are alternative forms of the names of King Isesi, see above. He is mentioned in an inscription from the 6th Dynasty tombs at Aswan, in it he is said to have sent to Punt for a dancing dwarf. Isesi's prenomen is given by the Saqqara List as Maatkare.

ELEPHANTINE

UNIS 5th Dynasty 2358-2328 BC

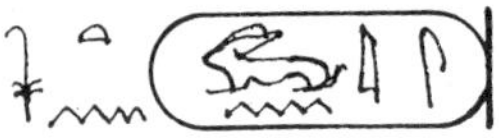

Sa Unis Unis

ONNUS, M. Inscription found on rocks at Elephantine. Pyramid at Saqqara, "The Pyramid which is Beautiful of Places". The sarcophagus found in the pyramid contained remains of a mummy which was probably his. Also known as Wenis. His pyramid was inscribed with some of the earliest known religious text.

Wadjtowe ELEPHANTINE

TETI 6th Dynasty 2328-2296 BC

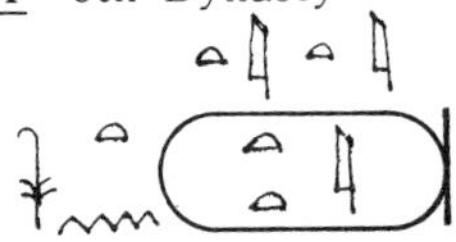

29
37

Teti Sa Teti

OTHOES - reigned 30 years. Murdered by his bodyguard, M. Founder of the new dynasty from Memphis. He built a pyramid at Saqqara, "The Pyramid which is Enduring of Places" or "The Prison Pyramid". Empty sarcophagus, but arm and shoulder of a mummy found.

Sheteptowe MEMPHIS

USERKARE 6th Dynasty 2296-2295 BC

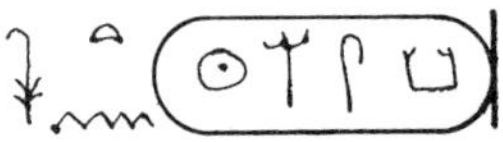

67

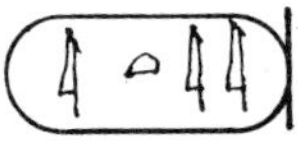

29

User ka Re Ity (Iti)

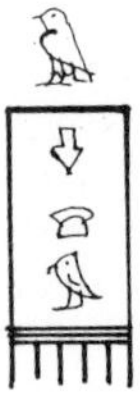

There is difficulty in identifying Userkare. He is not mentioned by Manetho, but is on the Abydos List after Teti. A Wadi Hammamat inscription concerns stone for Iti's pyramid, "The Pyramid of the Ba-spirits", location unknown. Some have identified Iti with Userkare, others with Teti. Others place him in the 7th/10th Dynasty.

Sekhemkhau MEMPHIS

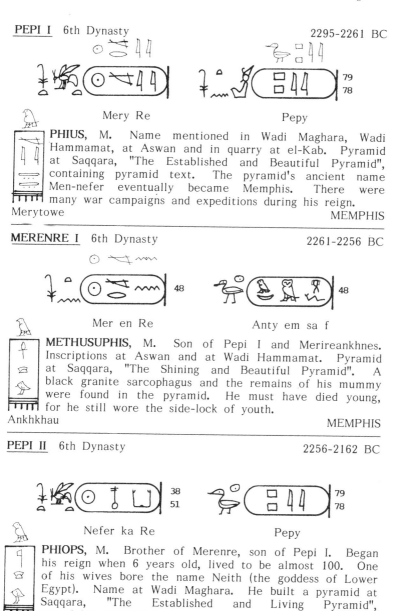

PEPI I 6th Dynasty 2295-2261 BC

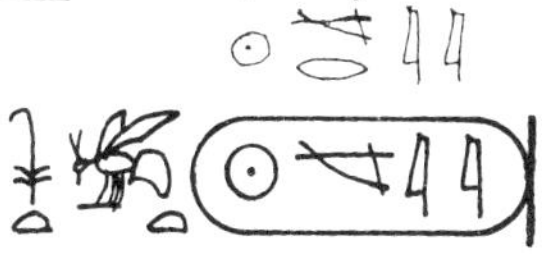

79
78

Mery Re

Pepy

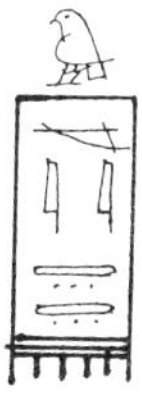

PHIUS, M. Name mentioned in Wadi Maghara, Wadi Hammamat, at Aswan and in quarry at el-Kab. Pyramid at Saqqara, "The Established and Beautiful Pyramid", containing pyramid text. The pyramid's ancient name Men-nefer eventually became Memphis. There were many war campaigns and expeditions during his reign.

Merytowe

MEMPHIS

MERENRE I 6th Dynasty 2261-2256 BC

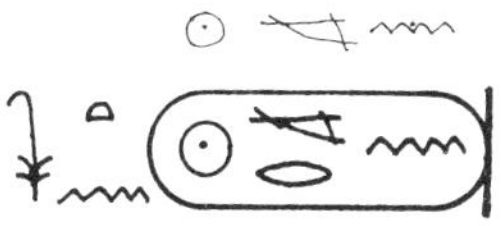

48

48

Mer en Re

Anty em sa f

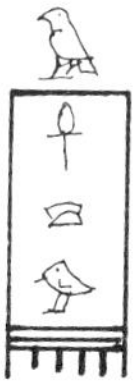

METHUSUPHIS, M. Son of Pepi I and Merireankhnes. Inscriptions at Aswan and at Wadi Hammamat. Pyramid at Saqqara, "The Shining and Beautiful Pyramid". A black granite sarcophagus and the remains of his mummy were found in the pyramid. He must have died young, for he still wore the side-lock of youth.

Ankhkhau

MEMPHIS

PEPI II 6th Dynasty 2256-2162 BC

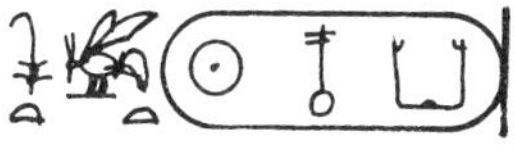

38
51

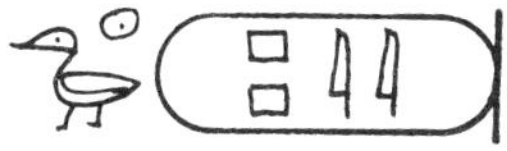

79
78

Nefer ka Re

Pepy

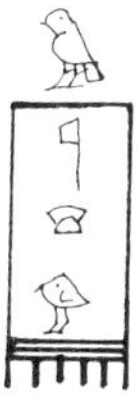

PHIOPS, M. Brother of Merenre, son of Pepi I. Began his reign when 6 years old, lived to be almost 100. One of his wives bore the name Neith (the goddess of Lower Egypt). Name at Wadi Maghara. He built a pyramid at Saqqara, "The Established and Living Pyramid", containing pyramid text.

Neterkhau

MEMPHIS

MERENRE II 6th Dynasty 2162-2161 BC

 47

Anty em sa f

MENTHESUPHIS - reigned only one year, killed in a riot but avenged by his sister/wife Queen Nitocris, M. His name is given by the Abydos List only and no monumental evidence has ever been found.

MEMPHIS

NITOCRIS Q 6th Dynasty 2161-2160 BC

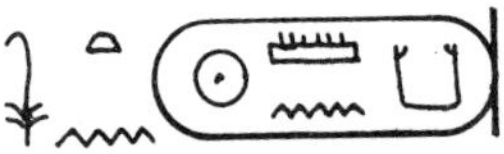 42 51

Men ka Re

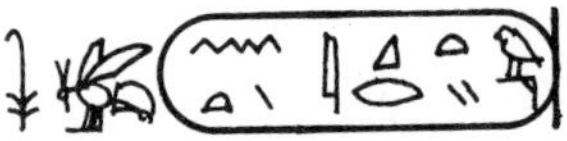 137

Net iqerty

NITOCRIS - the noblest and loveliest of women, reigned 12 years, M. Reputed to have committed suicide after avenging her brother Menthesuphis. She is said to have completed the pyramid of Menkaure and to have been buried in it.

MEMPHIS

IMHOTEP 6th Dynasty

Im hotep

IMHOTEP. This cartouche bears the name of a King Imhotep and was found in the Wadi Hammamat. He may have been contemporary with the 6th Dynasty or the First Intermediate Period.

MEMPHIS

4.05 REGISTER OF KINGS - FIRST INTERMEDIATE PERIOD
c 2160-2040 BC

7TH DYNASTY 2160-
(MEMPHIS)

2160	Neferka	51
	Nefer	51
	Neterkare	51
	Menkare	51
	Neferkare	51
	Neferkare-Neby	51
	Djedkare-Shemaat	51
	Neferkare-Khendu	51
	Merenhor	51
	Sneferka	51
	(Sneferkare)	51
	Nikare	51
	Neferkare-Tereru	51
	Neferkahor	51

8TH DYNASTY - 2140 BC
(MEMPHIS)

	Neferkare-Pepysonb		52
	Sneferka-Anu		52
	Kakare	Ibi	52
	Kakaure		52
	Neferkaure		52
	Neferkauhor		52
	Neferirkare		52
2140			

9TH/10TH DYNASTY 2140-2040 BC
(HERACLEOPOLIS)

2140	Neferkare		51
2134	Khety I	Meryibre	53
	Senen.h		52
		Neferkare	51
	Mery...	Kheti	52
	Sd...		52
2118	H...		52
2115	Khety II	Wahkare	53
2070	Merykare		53
	(Kameryre)		53
2069			
2061			
2040	Khety III	Nebkau	54

11TH DYNASTY 2134-2040 BC
(THEBES)

Inyotef-Hereditary Prince		54
Inyotef I	Horus Sehertowe	54
Inyotef II	Horus Wahankh	55
Inyotef III	Nakhtnebtepnufer	55
Mentuhotep	Nebhotepre	55

The Old Kingdom had been a great period in Egyptian history. The last five centuries had brought the sun-worshippers to the pinnacle of power - from now on every would-be king would claim descent from the Sun-God. However, the declining power of the Memphite kings of the 6th Dynasty resulted in calamity and chaos and the next twenty years saw about twenty minor Memphite kings, each struggling to keep control, but the line died out and the country was divided again.

A family from Heracleopolis now claimed the kingship in Middle Egypt, whilst at about the same time an hereditary prince from Thebes - Inyotef, emerged as a strong force, his descendants eventually claiming the throne for the South.

Over the centuries the Osiris cult had strengthened and spread. Nearby Abydos, became the Mecca of Osiris worship, and pilgrimages of both living and dead were made to it. It was everyone's wish, if not to be buried there, to at least visit it. Abydos blossomed as the religious centre of Egypt. The Osiris cult had once been the prerogative of the king only, but now it had become the right of everyone given by consent of the king. Upon death everyone had the opportunity to pass on to the fields of Osiris, the heaven granted to the right and just. The king as the Son of Re would enter upon death the barge of Re and join his father in his journeys across the sky.

Manetho's Kings List suggests that the Heracleopolitan royal family ruled all Egypt. This may have been so in the early part of the 9th Dynasty. Although the precise order of the royal family of Khety is not known, evidence of the probable first, King Meryibre Khety is widespread. The Inyotef princes however, quickly established themselves as kings at Thebes, and ruled as the 11th Dynasty, contemporary with the 9th and 10th Dynasties until about 2040 BC.

At this time the Inyotefs had been replaced by another Theban family - the Mentuhoteps, who were of the same blood line. They incorporated into their name, Mont (Mentu), the local god of Hermonthis near Thebes.

The struggle between the contemporary ruling kings intensified until the Theban, King Mentuhotep Nebhotepre, finally conquered the Heracleopolitans to bring unification again. At this point in his reign he changed his names to Nebhepetre, and Horus Samtowe - uniter of the two lands.

The sequence of kings of this period is derived from the Kings Lists. For studies on chronology of the period see the work of W A Ward (Bibliography)

7TH DYNASTY FROM MEMPHIS

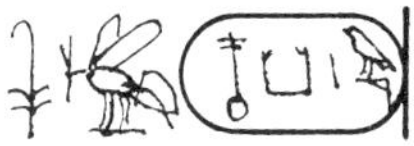

Nefer ka (a child)

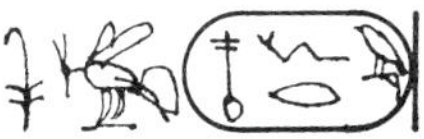

Nefer

Neter ka Re

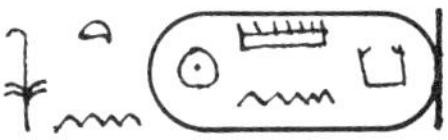

48

Men ka Re (Netiqerty)

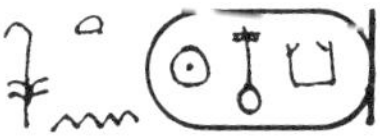

47
118

Nefer ka Re (also 9th Dyn)

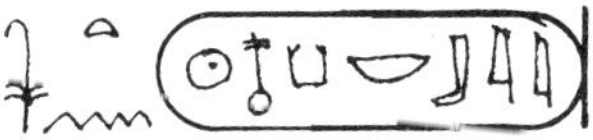

Nefer ka Re-Neby

Djed ka Re-Shemaat

Nefer ka Re-Khendu

Mer en Hor

80

Ni ka Re

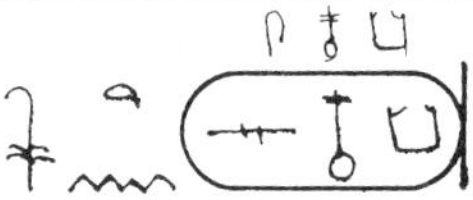

52

Snefer ka

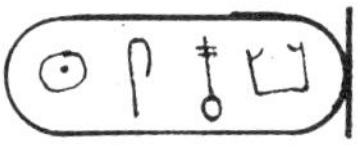

75

Snefer ka Re

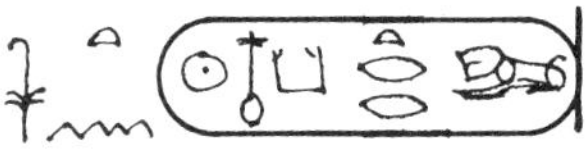

Nefer ka Re-Tereru

52

Nefer ka Hor

8TH DYNASTY FROM MEMPHIS

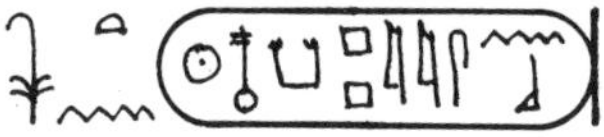

Nefer ka Re-Pepysonb

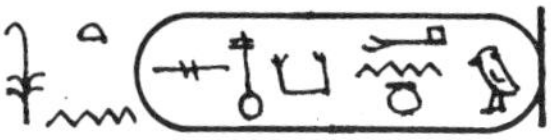

Snefer ka-Anu

KAKARE 8th Dynasty

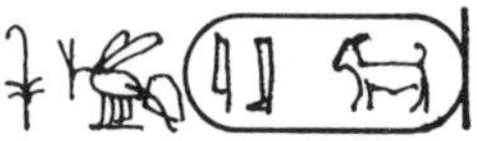

72

Ibi

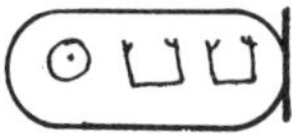

Ka ka Re

This king's name is on the Turin List, where he is given a reign of 4 years and 2 months. A ruined pyramid at Saqqara (Jaquies), is thought to have been started by him. He may be the Kakaure of the Abydos List.

MEMPHIS

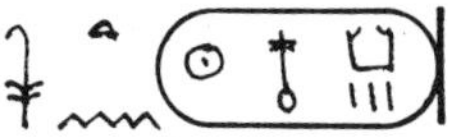

Nefer kau Re

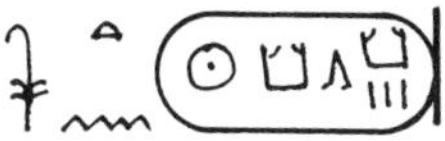

Ka kau Re

This king is referred to in decrees, for the protection of the Temple of Min at Koptos and others referring to court matters.

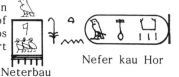

Neterbau

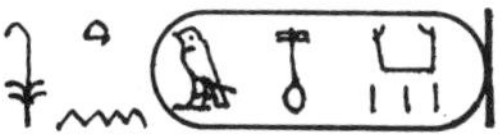

Nefer kau Hor

8TH DYNASTY

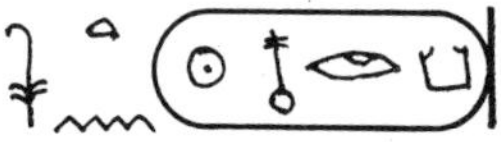

43

Nefer ir ka Re

9TH/10TH DYNASTY

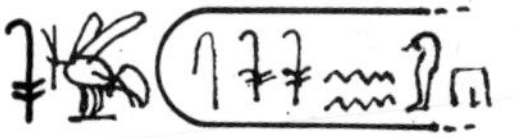

Senen.h

Sd...

9TH/10TH DYNASTY FROM HERACLEOPOLIS

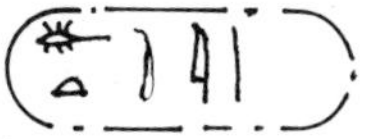

53

Mery... Kheti

H...

KHETY I 9th/10th Dynasty c 2134 BC

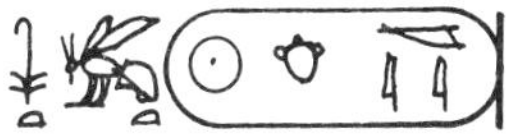

54

Mery ib Re Khety

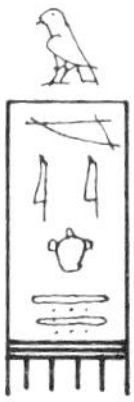

AKHTOY. **ACHTHOES** - more terrible than all kings before him, he did much evil unto the people of Egypt. Went mad and was destroyed by a crocodile, M. Not much known of him, but he claimed the kingship of all Egypt. His name was found on the rocks of the First Cataract and on an open copper-work basket, (Louvre).

Meryibtowe HERACLEOPOLIS

KHETY II 9th/10th Dynasty c 2115 BC

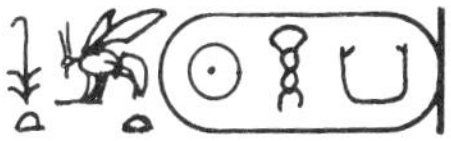

120

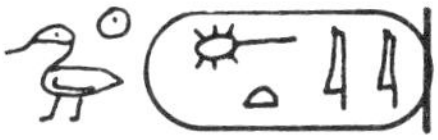

54

Wah ka Re Khety

AKHTOY. Little is known of this king, other than his name mentioned on the coffin of a steward at El-Bersha. He is probably the king who left instructions to his son Merykare, in which a condemnation of the Asiatic Beduin as the enemy of Egypt, is given. The instructions suggest that they were so - 'from the time of Horus'.

HERACLEOPOLIS

MERYKARE 9th/10th Dynasty c 2070 BC

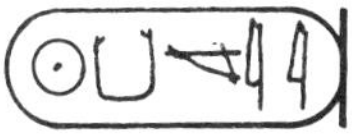

144

Mery ka Re (Kameryre)

Probably the son of Khety - Wahkare. He was engaged in battles against the Inyotefs of Thebes. After one particular skirmish in Upper Egypt, he ordered extensive repairs to the temple of Wepwawe, the jackal god of Assyut. He had a funerary cult at Heracleopolis, and a pyramid at Saqqara may be his.

HERACLEOPOLIS

KHETY III 9th/10th Dynasty c 2040 BC

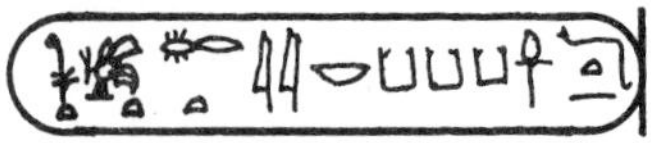
53

Neb kau Khety

AKHTOY. Little is known about this king but the story of the eloquent peasant dates from his time. The story, which comes from a document later used by scribes as a model, relates how a peasant suffered robbery by the employee of a feudal lord and was able to obtain justice by petitioning the king.

HERACLEOPOLIS

INYOTEF Hereditary Prince of Thebes 11th Dynasty

In yotef the Erpa

Probably the founder of the 11th Dynasty. He was the mighty chieftain of Upper Egypt 'Inyotef the Great'. Seen in the temple of Tod (near Thebes) making offerings to the god Mont, followed by the goddess Tjeniti and the next three kings of the dynasty, all named Inyotef.

THEBES

INYOTEF I 11th Dynasty 2134-2118 BC

55

In yotef

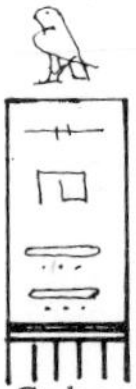
Sehertowe

ANTEF. His Horus name means "pacifier of the two lands", which suggests that the North was subdued. The Southern capital was now at Thebes and his pyramid tomb lies just to the south on the West Bank. Tombs of this period are mentioned in the Abbot Papyrus, referring to the tomb robberies of the New Kingdom.

THEBES

INYOTEF II 11th Dynasty 2118-2069 BC

54
86

54
86

In yotef In yotef

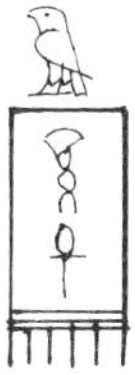

ANTEF. During the reign of Inyotefs the local god at Hermonthis near Thebes, was Mont. The lesser god of Thebes was Amon who later became god of all Egypt as Amon-Re (Amen-Re). Inyotef II captured the whole of the Abydos territory and opened up its prisons. He was a builder of temples and had a pyramid tomb at Thebes.

Wahankh THEBES

INYOTEF III 11th Dynasty 2069-2061 BC

54
86

In yotef

ANTEF. His Horus name translates as "strong lord beginning good", which may mean that the country was stable at the start of his reign. He ordered restoration work in the tombs at Aswan and had a pyramid tomb at Thebes. His son Mentuhotep I was eventually to claim kingship of all Egypt and begin the dominance by Thebes.

Nakhtnebtepnufer THEBES

MENTUHOTEP I 11th Dynasty 2061-2010 BC

57

57
58

Neb hotep Re Mentu hotep

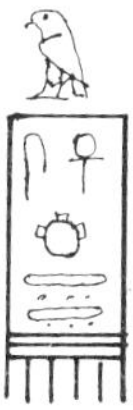

MENTUHOTPE. Son of Inyotef III, his name means 'Mont is content'. His long reign probably consolidated the union of the two lands under one king again. His Horus name translates as "life giving heart of the two lands". He built a temple at Deir el Bahri next to which the 18th Dynasty Queen, Hatshepsut, later built hers.

Sankhibtowe THEBES

4.06 REGISTER OF KINGS - MIDDLE KINGDOM

c 2040–1784 BC

11TH DYNASTY 2040-1962 BC (THEBES) ALL EGYPT

2061	Mentuhotep I	Horus Sankhibtowe	55
2040	Mentuhotep I	Nebhotepre	57
	Divine Father	Inyotef	nc
2010	Mentuhotep II	Sankhkare	57
	Divine Father	Senwosre	nc
1998	Mentuhotep III	Nebtowere	57
1991	Mentuhotep IV	Skha...re	58
1991	Amenemhet I	Shotepibre	58

12TH DYNASTY 1962-1783 BC (THEBES)

1962	Amenemhet I	Shotepibre	58
1971	Senwosre I	Kheperkare	58
1929	Amenemhet II	Nubkaure	59
1897	Senwosre II	Khakheperre	59
1878	Senwosre III	Khakaure	59
1843	Amenemhet III	Nimaatre	60
	Auibre	Hor	60
1798	Amenemhet IV	Maatkherure	60
1787	Sebekneferu Q	Sebekkare	61

The Theban family of Mentuhotep had now gained full control of all Egypt and the 11th Dynasty continued under their rule. The last King Nebtowere was not considered to have a rightful claim to the throne and he was usurped by his Vizier Amenemhet I, who began the 12th Dynasty.

The Amenemhet family ruled all Egypt for a further 178 years, the last of them being Queen Sebekneferu, sister of Amenemhet IV. Her brief reign indicates the demise of the blood line. It had been a great period in Egypt's history, but chaos was to follow.

MENTUHOTEP I 11th Dynasty 2061-2010 BC

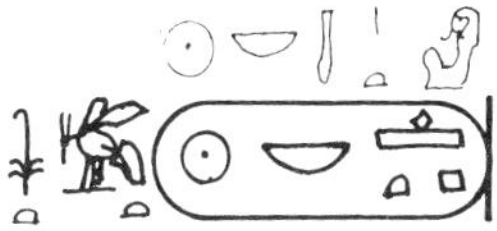 55

 55 58

Neb hotep Re Mentu hotep

MENTUHOTPE. In establishing his claim to sovereignty of first the South, then of all Egypt, he changed his names to Nebhepetre, Horus Neterhedje and finally to Horus Samtowe, 'Uniter of the Two Lands'. He was later considered by the Thebans to be a mighty king like Menes.

Neterhedje - Samtowe THEBES

MENTUHOTEP II 11th Dynasty 2010-1998 BC

 55 58

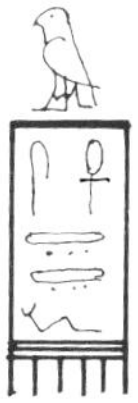

S ankh ka Re Mentu hotep

MENTUHOTPE. Son of Mentuhotep I. The main events in this king's reign are inscribed on the rocks at Wadi Hammamat. An expedition to Punt, the digging of some wells and a tablet showing him on the throne with his dogs lying at his feet. He lived most of his life under the reign of his father.

Sankhtowef THEBES

MENTUHOTEP III 11th Dynasty 1998-1991 BC

 55 58

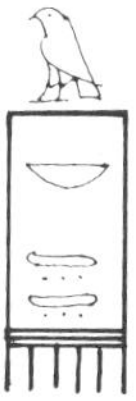

Neb towe Re Mentu hotep

MENTUHOTPE. Probably a weak king not regarded as the legitimate sovereign. The Turin Canon indicates a kingless period at this time. The vizier Amenemhe, son of a certain non-royal Senwosre, probably laid claim to the throne to become the next king.

Nebtowe THEBES

MENTUHOTEP IV 11th Dynasty c 1991 BC

 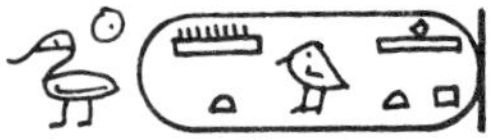 57 71

Skha . . . Re Mentu hotep

MENTUHOTPE. This king is unlikely to have come to the throne as a genuine ruler. He seems to have been usurped by Mentuhotep III's vizier Amenemhe, who was to seize the throne and start the 12th Dynasty as Manetho's Ammenemes.

THEBES

AMENEMHET I 12th Dynasty 1991-1971 BC

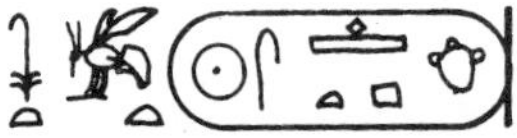 65  59 60

Shotep ib Re Amen em het

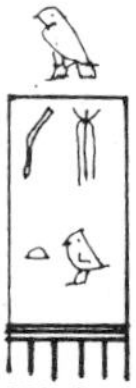

AMENEMHE. **AMMENEMES**, M. Manetho obliquely refers to him as a ruler, perhaps confirming his non-royal descent. He named his son Senwosre, thus immortalising his father's name as a king. He moved the capital to Lisht and built a pyramid there. From this period the God Amun begins to take preference to the God Mont.

Wehammeswe THEBES

SENWOSRE I 12th Dynasty 1971-1927 BC

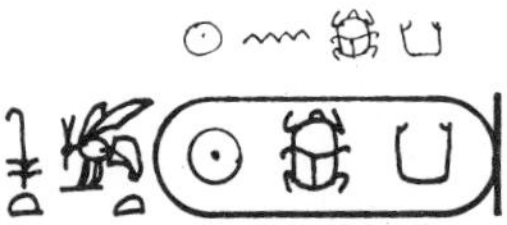 135 145 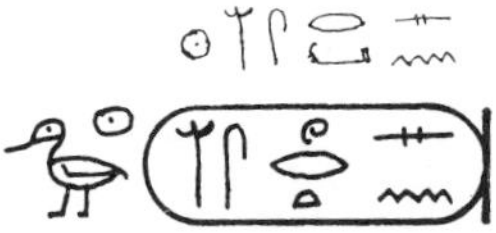 59 71

Kheper ka Re Sen wosre

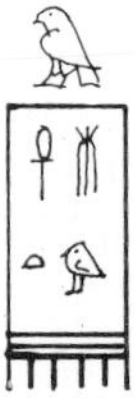

USERTEN. **SESONCHOSIS**, M. Son of Amenemhet I, he co-reigned with his father for 10 years. He refounded the Great Temple of the Sun at Heliopolis. He set up a granite oblisk in the Fayyum and is represented on it worshipping various gods. Built temples at Tanis, Abydos and Karnak. He had a pyramid at Lisht.

Ankhmeswe THEBES

AMENEMHET II 12th Dynasty 1929-1895 BC

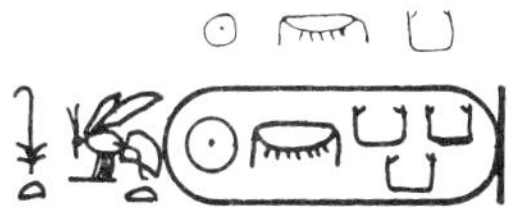

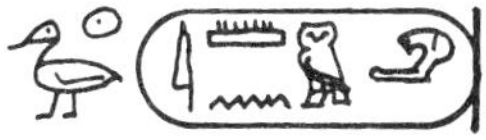

58
60

Nub kau Re — Amen em het

AMENEMHE. **AMMANEMES**, M. Son of Sesonchosis. He was murdered by his own eunuchs according to Manetho, but this may refer to his grandfather Ammenemes I. He co-reigned with his father for 2 years. Name on objects in a rich treasure of gold, silver and lapis lazuli, found at Tod. Trade between Egypt and Punt is recorded.

Hekenemmaat — THEBES

SENWOSRE II 12th Dynasty 1897-1878 BC

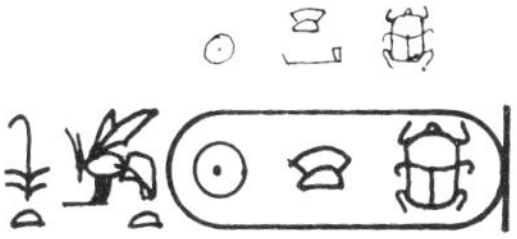

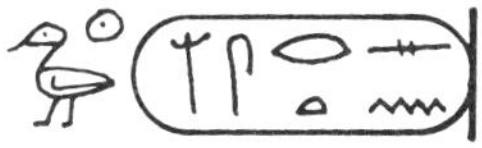

58
71

Kha kheper Re — Sen wosre

USERTEN. **SESOSTRIS** - reigned 48 years and conquered all Asia in 9 years, and Europe as far as Thrace, M. A statue of his wife Nefert was found at Tanis. He had a pyramid at Lahun, "The Shining Pyramid". This contained a white limestone altar of Osiris, which was set before his red granite sarcophagus.

Seshemutowe — THEBES

SENWOSRE III 12th Dynasty 1878-1841 BC

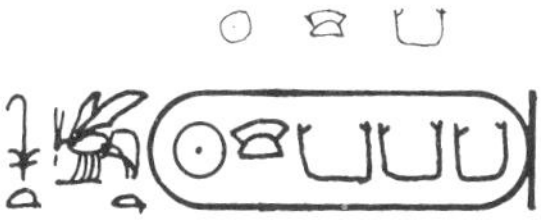

69

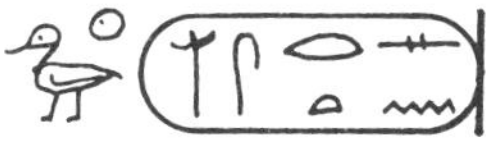

58
71

Kha kau Re — Sen wosre

USERTEN. **SESOSTRIS**, M. Waged war against the Nubians and reduced them to a pitiful state. A stele at the Second Cataract forbids any negro from passing into Egypt, except for trade or barter. He built a canal at the First Cataract, later re-dug by Tuthmosis III. Pyramid at Dahshur.

Neterkheperu — THEBES

AMENEMHET III 12th Dynasty 1843-1797 BC

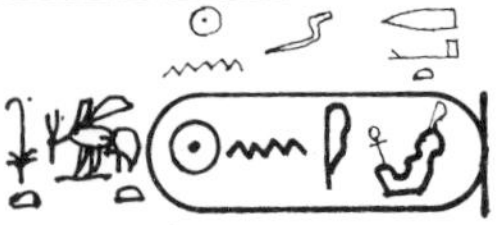

67

59
64

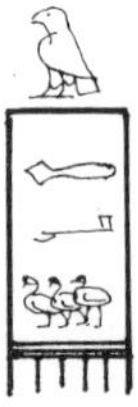

Ni Maat Re

Amen em het

AMENEMHE. **LACHARES,** M. Made the Great Lake Moeris in the Fayyum. Built the labyrinth funerary temple with his pyramid at Hawara. He had another pyramid at Dahshur. A statue of his was usurped by Merenptah (Dynasty 19), (Berlin Museum). His colossal statues once looked out over Lake Moeris from Biyahmu.

Abau

THEBES

AUIBRE 12th Dynasty INTERREGNUM

67
74

67

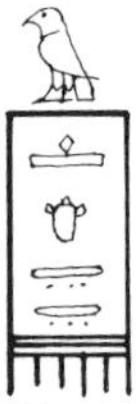

Au ib Re

Hor

From evidence in his tomb at Dahshur (De Morgan), he may be the brother or son of Amenemhet III and thus possibly Manetho's Ameres. However, Auibre must have died first thus another son Amenemhet IV became the next king. He may however, be the Auibre placed in the 13th Dynasty by the Turin Canon.

Hotepibtowe

THEBES

AMENEMHET IV 12th Dynasty 1798-1787 BC

59
64

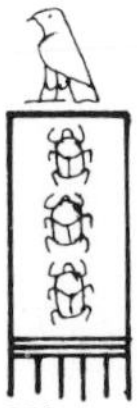

Maat kheru Re

Amen em het

AMENEMHE. **AMMENEMES,** M. Son of Amenemhet III, he probably co-reigned with his father for a while. His name is inscribed on the rocks at Wadi Maghara, and at the Second Cataract recording the height of the Nile. Otherwise nothing is known of this king, but his name is recorded in the Turin List with a reign of 12 years.

Kheperkheperu

THEBES

SEBEKNEFERU Q 12th Dynasty 1787-1783 BC

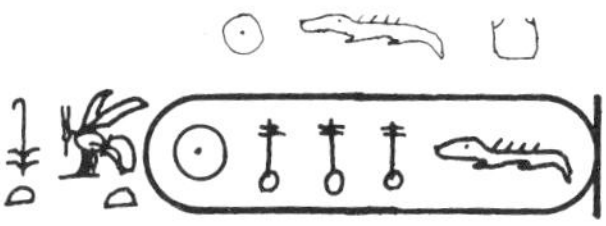

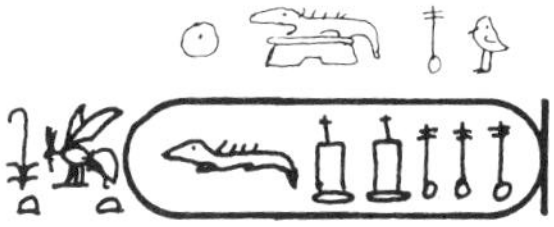

Sebek Ka Re
Neferu Sebek Re

Sebek neferu

SOBEKNEFERU. NEFERUSOBEK. **SCEMIOPHRIS.** Sister of **AMMENEMES,** reigned 4 years, M. Very little is known of this Queen. She obviously claimed the throne upon there being no male successor to Amenemhet IV. She honoured the crocodile God Sebek in her cartouches.

Meretre

THEBES

Amenemhet III
Alternative cartouche. See page 60

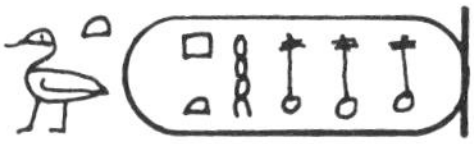

Ptahneferu
Wife of Amenemhet III

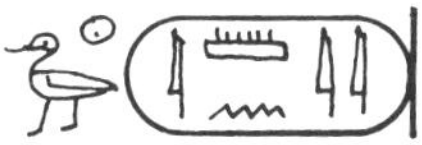

Ameni
(a Prince)

4.07 REGISTER OF KINGS - SECOND INTERMEDIATE PERIOD

c 1785-1554 BC

13TH DYNASTY 1785-1652 BC (THEBES)

1785	Wegaf	Khutowere	64
1783	Amenemhet (Sonbef)	Sekhemkare	64
1777	Pentini	Sekhemre khutowe	64
1777	Amenemhet V	Sekhemkare	64
1775	Sehotepibre	Sehotepibenre	65
1774	Efni		65
1773	Amenemhet VI (Amenyinyotef)	Seankhibre	65
1772	Semenkare	Iby	65
1770	Hornedhotef	Sehotepibre	66
1768	Ameny Kemu	Swadjkare	66
1766	Khuiqre	Nedjemibre	66
1764	Sebekhotep I	Khaankhre	66
1762	Renisonbe		66
1760	Auibre	Hor	67
1758	KayAmenemhet VII	Sedjefakare	67
1756	Sebekhotep II (Amenemhet)	Sekhemre khutowe	67
1754	Khendjer	Userkare nimaatre	67
1750	Mermashau	Smenkhkare	68
1747	Inyotef IV	...kare	68
1747	Nerkare	Hotepkare	68
1744	Aqen	...ibreset	68
1744	Sebekhotep III	Sekhemre sewadjtowe	68
1741	Neferhotep I	Khasekhemre	69
1730	Khakare	Sithathor	69
1730	Sebekhotep IV	Khaneferre	69
1720	Sebekhotep V	Khahotepre	69
1715	Ibiya	Wahibre	70
1704	Iya	Merneferre	70
1680	Sebekhotep VI	Merhotepre	70
1680	Ina (An)		70
1678	Seankhenre	Swadjtu	70
1675	Neferhotep II	Mersekhemre	70
1672	Swadjkare	Hori	71
1667	Sebekhotep VII	Merkaure	71
1665	Mentuhotep V	Merankhre	71
1664	Mentuemsaf	Djedankhre	71
1664	Senwosre IV	Sneferibre	71
1663	Dedumose I	Djedhotepre	71
1663	Dedumose II	Djedneferre	72
1662	Ibi	...matre	72
1660	Hor II	...ubenre	72
1660	Se...kare		72
1659	Senebmau	Sewahenre	72
1658	Sebekhotep VIII	Sekhemre seusertowe	72
1657	Sekhaenre		72
1656	Ini	Mershepsesre	73
1655	Merkheperre		73
1655	Merkare		73
1654	Neferhotep III	Sekhemre sankhtowe	73
1653	Seshib (Senaib)	Menkhaure	73
1653	Ipwatemsaf	Sekhemneferkhaure	73
1652	Mentuuserre		73

14TH DYNASTY 1715-1650 BC (XOIS)

Nehasi	74	Menibre	75
Khatire	74	Djed...re	75
Nebfaure	74	Ink...	75
Shebre	74	Ineb	76
Merdjefare	74	Ip	76
Swadjkare	74	Hibi (Ibis)	76
Nebdjefare	74	Aped (Sa)	76
...webenre	74	Hape (Apis)	76
...djefare	74	Shemes	76
Webenre	74	Meni	76
Auibre	74	Werqa	76
Heribre	74	Seth	76
Nebsenre	74	Shanu...	76
Skheperenre	75	Hor	76
Djedkherure	75	Eniben	76
Sankhibre	75	Pensetin...	76
Nefertemkare	75	Kherhimut	76
Sekhem...re	75	Khuhim...	76
Kakemure	75	Swadjenre	76
Neferibre	75		
Ya...	75		
Kha...re	75		
Akare	75		
Smen...re	75		
Djed...re	75		
Sneferkare	75		

14TH DYNASTY (XOIS) contemporary with the **13TH DYNASTY** from:-
1715 to 1650 BC

17TH DYNASTY 1652-1554 BC (THEBES)

1652	Inyotef V	Nubkheperre	81
1647	Rehotep	Sekhemre wahkhau	81
1644	Sebekemsaf I	Sekhemre wadjkhau	81
1628	Dhuti	Sekhemre smentowe	82
1627	Mentuhotep VI	Seankhenre	82
1626	Nebiriaure I	Sewadjenre	82
1607	Nebiriaure II	Neferkare	83
1607	Smenenre		83
1606	Seuserenre		83
1594	Sebekemsaf II	Sekhemre shedtowe	84
1585	Inyotef VI	Sekhemre wepmaat	84
1580	Inyotef VII	Sekhemre herhimaat	84
1580	Ta'o I	Senakhtenre	85
1575	Ta'o II	Seqenenre	85
1560	Kamose	Wadjkheperre	85
1553			

15TH DYNASTY 1652-1544 BC (SAITE)

Sharek	Sekhaenre	77
Sheshi	Maatibre	77
Iquebher	Meruserre	77
Khian	Seuserenre	77
Apopi I	Auserre	78
Apopi II	Akenenre	78
Apopi III	Nebkhepeshre	78
Khamudi	Asehre	79

16TH DYNASTY
28 minor kings - contemporary with the **15TH DYNASTY** from:-
1650 to 1552 BC
(See page 79/80)

In a now familiar way, the decline of the strong early part of the Middle Kingdom had resulted in very weak minor kingships, leaving Egypt vulnerable to almost any strong outsider. It was in this period of dissolution that the 13th Dynasty rulers were being challenged by other minor contemporary kings of the 14th Dynasty.

The emergence of the Hyksos kings of the 15th Dynasty, left a lasting scar on the memory of later Egyptians. The word Hyksos seems to mean 'Chief of a foreign land', and this has been interpreted by many as representing a whole-scale invasion of Egypt by these Hyksos people. A favourable alternative is however, that the people of whom the Hyksos kings belonged were long established foreigners in Egypt, and that they took advantage of the weakness of Egypt to size control. An invasion from within by contemporary foreigners.

The rise of the Hyksos ousted the contemporary 13th Dynasty Diospolites (Theban) and 14th Dynasty (Delta) reigns, and although ruling from Memphis, seems to have reached all parts of the country.

Their rule however, was not uncontested. Contemporaneous with them, the 17th Dynasty Theban princes claimed kingship and bitterly opposed them.

In a similar manner the 16th Dynasty ran concurrent. A series of minor kings, also of foreign extract, usually referred to as minor Hyksos kings. They were probably local governors tolerated by the main kings.

It was the militant Thebans who were to end the Hyksos dominance. They were finally driven out by King Ahmose whose family had risen to power in Thebes and had fought many battles with the foreign rulers.

Ahmose was revered by the Thebans as founder of the mighty New Kingdom and was placed alongside MENES and MENTUHOTEP, as glorious unifiers of the two lands.

Of the kings themselves very little is known, for most of them only their name has survived.

The sequence of the kings of this period is determined mainly from the Turin Canon. The chronology agrees basically with that of Jurgen Von Beckerath (see Bibliography).

WEGAF 13th Dynasty 1785-1783 BC

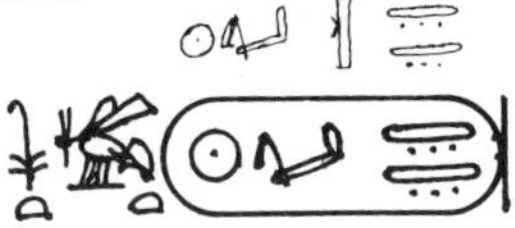

Khu towe Re — Wegaf

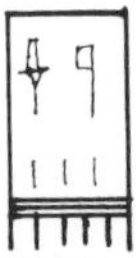

According to the Turin Canon this king begins a new period. Not mentioned in the Aydos and Saqqara Lists, but appears in the Karnak one. He probably came from Thebes. Name on a statuette (Khartoum Museum), an inscription at Medamud and a stele from Karnak.

Sekhemneteru

THEBES

AMENEMHET - SONBEF 13th Dynasty c 1783 BC

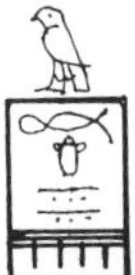

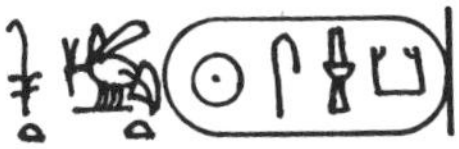

86
144

Sekhem ka Re — Amen em het-Sonbef

Mehibtowe

THEBES

PENTINI 13th Dynasty c 1777 BC

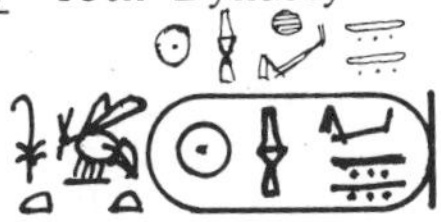

67

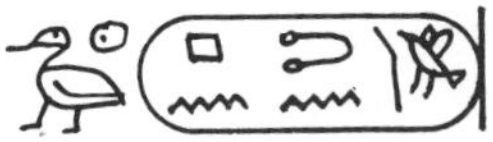

Sekhem Re-khu towe — Pentini

Khabau

THEBES

AMENEMHET V 13th Dynasty 1777-1775 BC

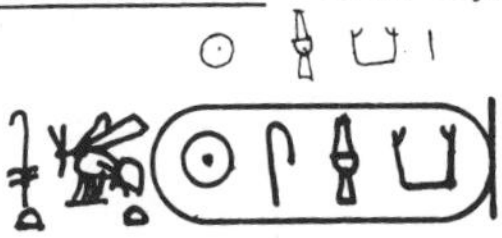

86
144

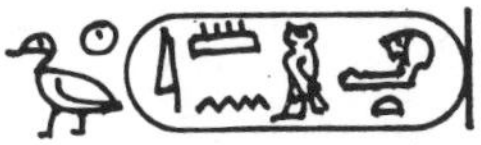

60

Sekhem ka Re — Amen em het

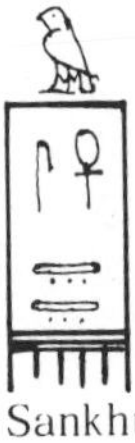

AMENEMHE. Although this king's Horus name means 'Revivor of the Two Lands', little is known of him. A stele from Athribis (Delta) shows Hapy the Nile God, making offerings to him, with Horus of Edfu the winged disk of the Sun also present. Fragments of statues are inscribed with the two names.

Sankhtowe

THEBES

SEHOTEPIBRE 13th Dynasty 1775-1774 BC

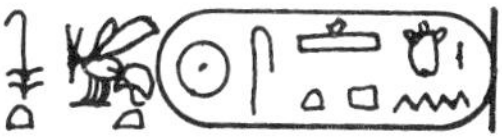

Sehotep ib en Re

58
66

Sehotep ib Re

EFNI 13th Dynasty c 1774 BC

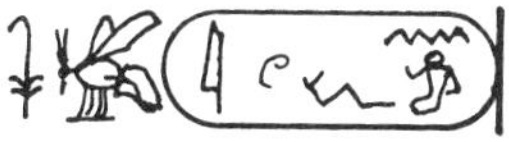

Efni

AMENEMHET VI 13th Dynasty c 1773 BC

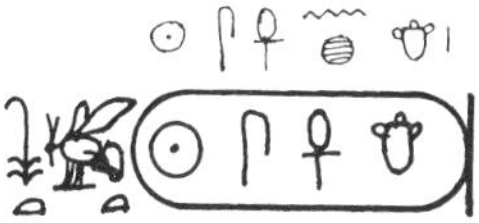

Seankh ib Re

(Ameny Inyotef)
Amen em het

A large table of offerings inscribed with his name was discovered at Karnak. His Horus name means 'Pacifier of the Two Lands'. His name was also found on a cylinder seal.

Sehertowe

THEBES

SEMENKARE 13th Dynasty c 1772 BC

Iby

Semen ka Re

Semenkare is listed on the Turin Canon and Iby is referred to on the Memphis Priest List as reigning during this period, but these may be two separate kings.

THEBES

HORNEDJHERTEF 13th Dynasty c 1770 BC

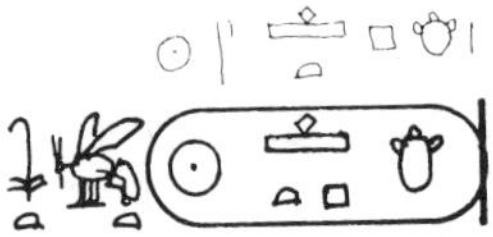 65

(Se) Hotep ib Re — Kemu Si Hor nedj her tef

Name on the Turin Canon and on blocks from the Temple of Anty at el Atawla (Middle Egypt). A sitting figure found at Tell ed Daba (Delta), bears his name and that of the God Ptah.

AMENY KEMU - Swadjkare 13th Dynasty c 1768 BC

 71 74

Ameny kemu — Swadj ka Re

These may be two separate kings.

KHUIQRE - Nedjemibre 13th Dynasty c 1766 BC

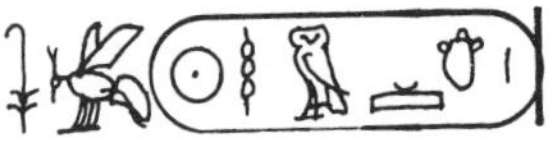

Khu iqre — Nedjem ib Re

These may be two separate kings.

SEBEKHOTEP I 13th Dynasty c 1764 BC

 67 68

Kha ankh Re — Sebek hotep

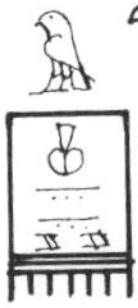

Smatowe

His power extended over the two lands. Name on a granite altar from Abydos, stele, base of a statue, blocks from the Temple of Mentuhotep (Deir el Bahri).

THEBES

RENISONBE 13th Dynasty c 1762 BC

Reni sonbe

Name on Turin Canon only.

AUIBRE 13th Dynasty c 1760 BC

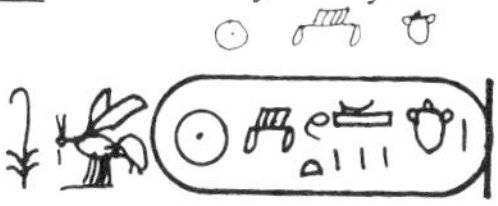
60
74

60

Au ib Re Hor

From the Turin Canon, but see page 60.

KAY AMENEMHET VII 13th Dynasty c 1758 BC

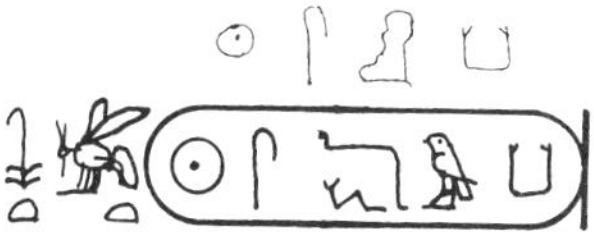

Sedjefa ka Re Ka Amen em het

Inscription found in the tomb of Queen Khuit at Saqqara. Other items bear his name, including cylinder seals and scarabs.

Herteptowe

AMENEMHET - Sebekhotep II 13th Dynasty c 1756 BC

Sekhem Re-khu towe Amen em het

Name found on various items:- cylinder seal, fragments of statues, architraves, scarabs, and papyrus inscriptions.

KHENDJER 13th Dynasty c 1754 BC

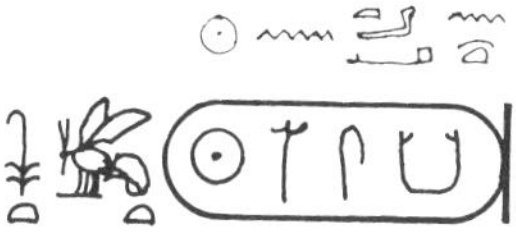
60
46

User ka Re-Ni maat Re Khen djer

He built a pyramid at Saqqara, which gives Userkare. Stele from Abydos gives Nimaatre (Louvre). Cylinder seals and scarabs.

MERMASHAU 13th Dynasty c 1750 BC

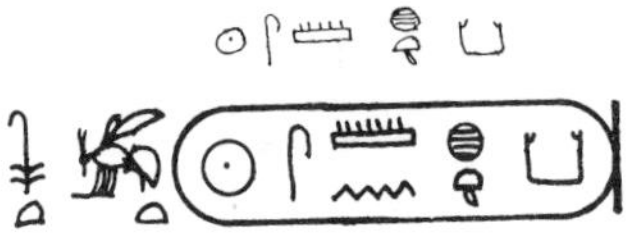

93
94

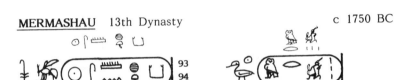

Smenkh ka Re — Mer mashu

Two granite statues from Temple of Ptah (Tanis). The General of the priest of Mendes.

INYOTEF IV 13th Dynasty c 1747 BC

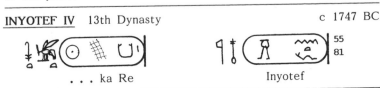

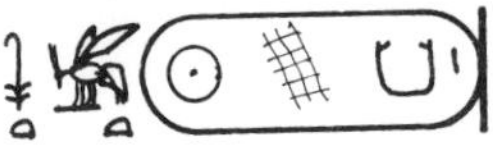

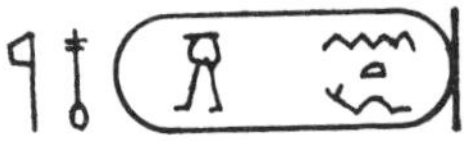

55
81

. . . ka Re — Inyotef

NERKARE-HOTEPKARE 13th Dynasty c 1747 BC

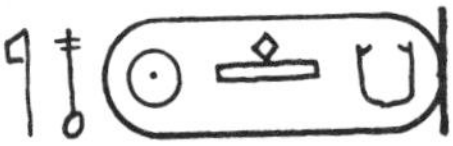

Ner ka Re — Hotep ka Re

One of these kings is perhaps the throne name of Inyotef above. Names found on cylinder seals and scarabs.

AQEN 13th Dynasty c 1744 BC

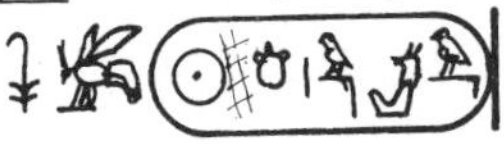

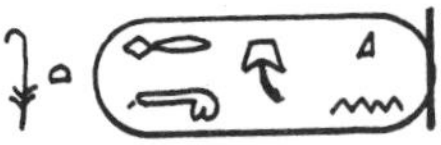

. . . ib Re Set — Aqen

SEBEKHOTEP III 13th Dynasty 1744-1741 BC

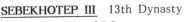

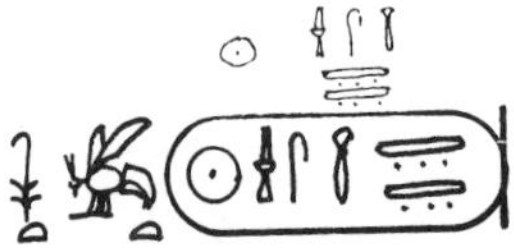

67
69

Sekhem Re - sewadj towe — Sebek hotep

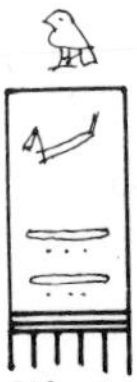

Khutowe

Son of the 'Divine Father' Mentuhotep and the 'Royal Mother' Auhetibu. He is thus named on a stele from Koptos. Other items bear his name:- a small oblisk from Karnak, a statue from Bubastis, cylinder seals, scarabs etc. The Turin Canon and the Karnak List confirm his reign.

THEBES

NEFERHOTEP I 13th Dynasty 1741-1730 BC

70
73

Kha sekhem Re Nefer hotep

Son of a 'Divine Father' (a non-royal), and a 'Royal Mother'. He thus gained the throne by his mother's royal blood. His Horus name means 'Pacifier of the Two Lands'. A number of other items carry his names, and a statuette of him stands in Bologna Museum.

Hoteptowe

THEBES

KHAKARE 13th Dynasty c 1730 BC

Kha ka Re Sit hathor

Son of Neferhotep I. According to the Turin Canon he reigned for only 2 months.

SEBEKHOTEP IV 13th Dynasty 1730-1720 BC

68
70

Kha nefer Re Sebek hotep

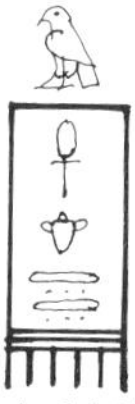

He was the brother of Neferhotep I - Khasekhemre and co-reigned with him. A great king whose reign was widespread. Colossal statues of him were found at Tanis and other statues on the Island of Argo, near the Third Cataract. Other items bear his name, including a large stele from Abydos, scarabs and cylinder seals.

Ankhibtowe

THEBES

SEBEKHOTEP V 13th Dynasty 1720-1715 BC

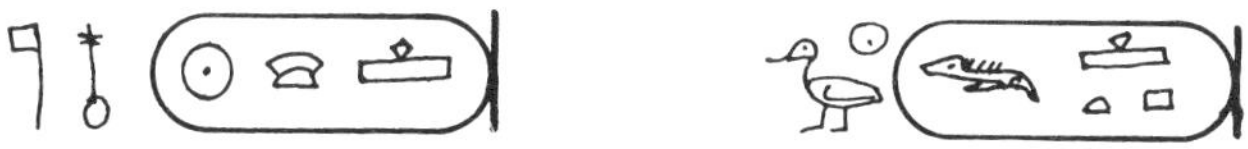

68
70

Kha hotep Re Sebek hotep

THEBES

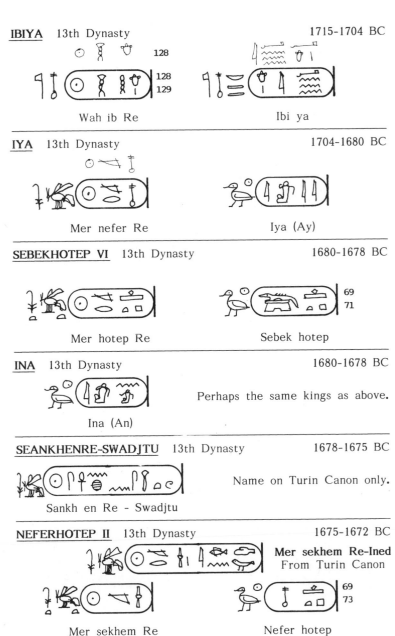

IBIYA 13th Dynasty 1715-1704 BC

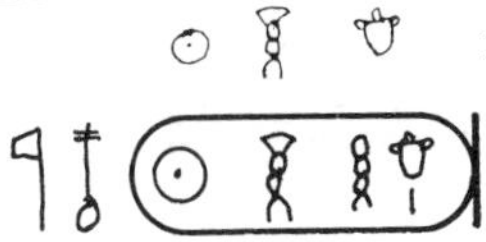

128
128
129

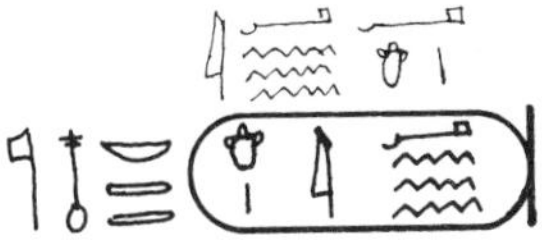

Wah ib Re — Ibi ya

IYA 13th Dynasty 1704-1680 BC

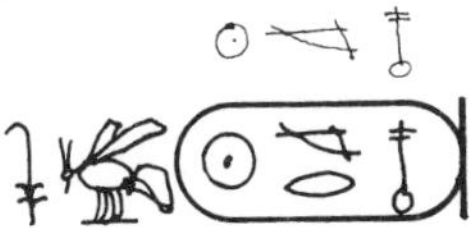

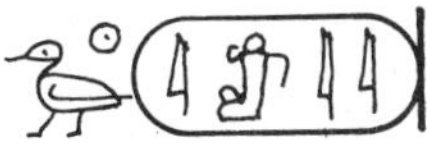

Mer nefer Re — Iya (Ay)

SEBEKHOTEP VI 13th Dynasty 1680-1678 BC

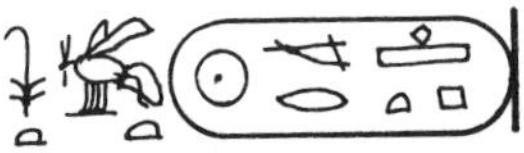

69
71

Mer hotep Re — Sebek hotep

INA 13th Dynasty 1680-1678 BC

Ina (An)

Perhaps the same kings as above.

SEANKHENRE-SWADJTU 13th Dynasty 1678-1675 BC

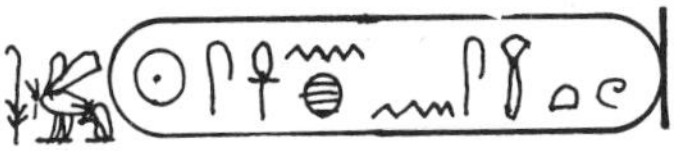

Sankh en Re - Swadjtu

Name on Turin Canon only.

NEFERHOTEP II 13th Dynasty 1675-1672 BC

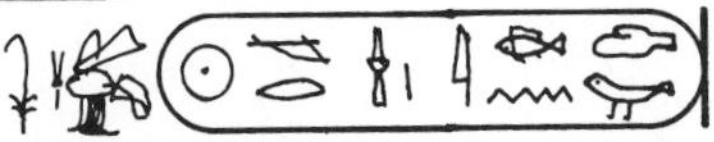

Mer sekhem Re-Ined
From Turin Canon

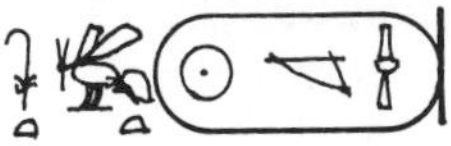

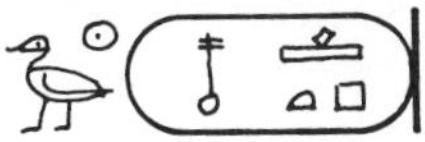

69
73

Mer sekhem Re — Nefer hotep

SWADJKARE 13th Dynasty 1672-1667 BC

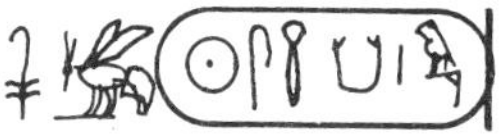

66
74

Swadj ka Re

Hori

SEBEKHOTEP VII 13th Dynasty 1667-1665 BC

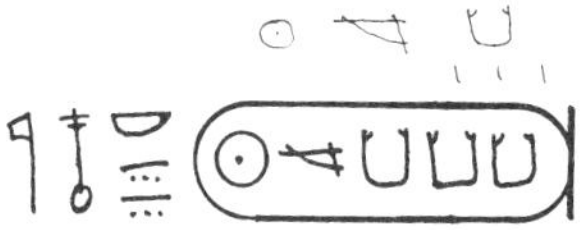

Mer kau Re

70
72

Sebek hotep

MENTUHOTEP V 13th Dynasty 1665-1664 BC

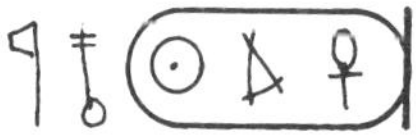

Mer ankh Re

58
02

Mentu hotep

MENTUEMSAF 13th Dynasty c 1664 BC

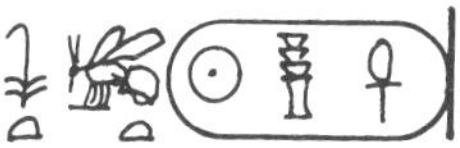

Djed ankh Re

Mentu em saf

SENWOSRE IV 13th Dynasty c 1664 BC

Snefer ib Re

86
59

Sen wosre

Horus Beankh

DEDUMOSE I 13th Dynasty c 1663 BC

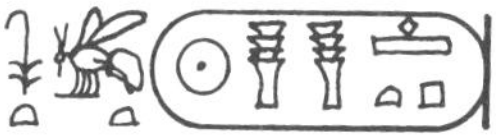

Djed hotep Re

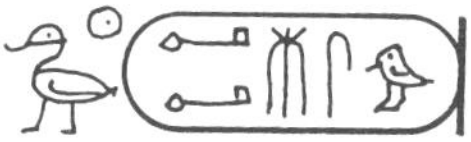

Dedu mose

Horus Wadjkha

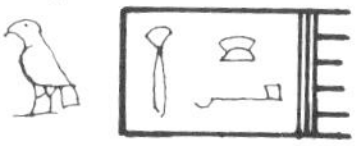

DEDUMOSE II 13th Dynasty c 1663 BC

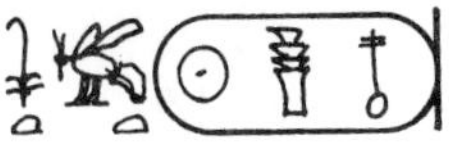

Djed nefer Re

 71

Dedu mose

IBI 13th Dynasty c 1662 BC

. . . maat Re

 52

Ibi

HOR 13th Dynasty

. . . uben Re-Hor

SE . . . KARE c 1660 BC

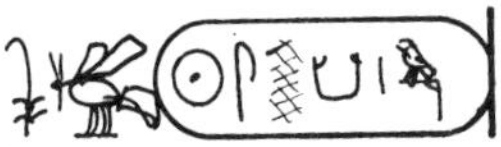

Se . . . ka Re

SENEBMAU 13th Dynasty c 1659 BC

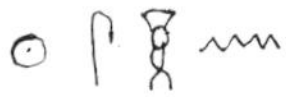

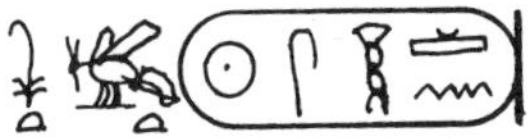

Sewah en Re

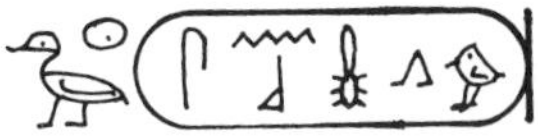

Seneb mau

SEBEKHOTEP VIII 13th Dynasty c 1658 BC

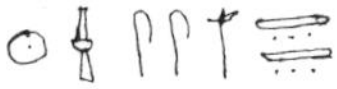

Sekhem Re-Seuser towe

 70 71

Sebek hotep

SEKHAENRE 13th Dynasty c 1657 BC

Sekha en Re

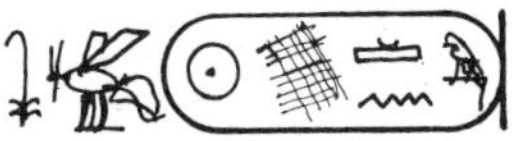

Sekha en Re

INI 13th Dynasty c 1656 BC

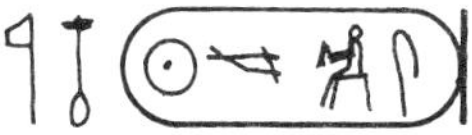

Mer shepses Re

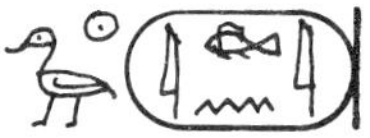
44

Ini

MERKHEPERRE 13th Dynasty **MERKARE** 13th Dyn c 1655 BC

Mer kheper Re

Mer ka Re

NEFERHOTEP III 13th Dynasty c 1654 BC

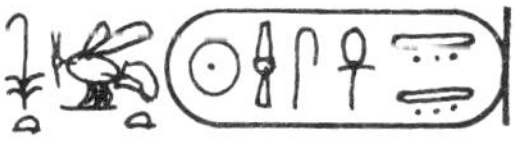

Sekhem Re sankh towe

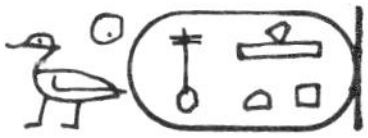
69
70

Nefer hotep

Horus Wadjkhau 

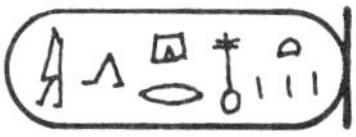

SESHIB 13th Dynasty c 1653 BC

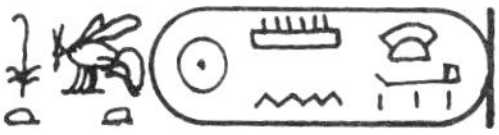

Men khau Re

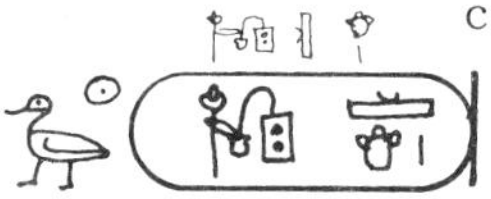

Sesh ib (Sena ib)

Horus Swadjtowe 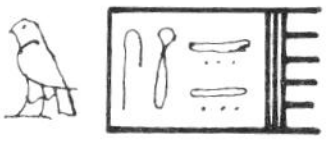

IPWATEMSAF 13th Dynasty c 1653 BC

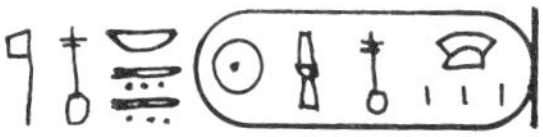

Sekhem nefer khau Re

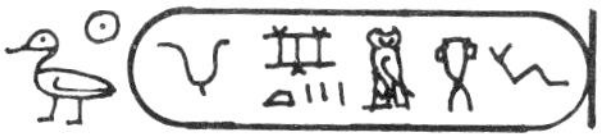

Ip wat em sa f

MENTUUSERRE 13th Dynasty c 1652 BC

Mentu user Re

14TH DYNASTY FROM XOIS c 1715-1650 BC

Ne hasi

87

Ne hasy

A colossal black granite statue of the king seated. In an inscription at Tanis he is called Royal Son firstborn Nehsi. Worshipper of Set.

Kha ti Re (Kha ty Re)

Neb f au Re
Reigned approx 1 year

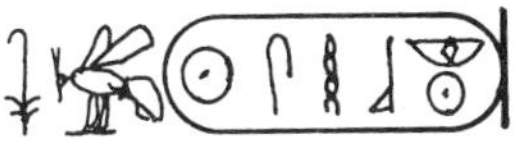

Sheb Re
Reigned approx 3 years

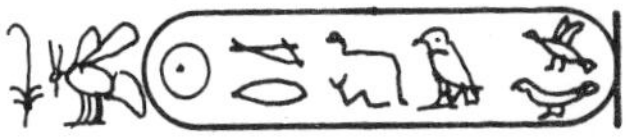

Mer djefa Re
Reigned approx 3 years

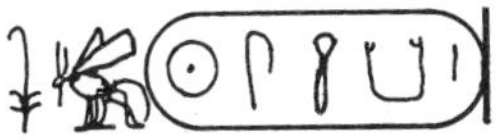

66
71

Swadj ka Re
Reigned approx 1 year

Neb djefa Re
Reigned approx 1 year

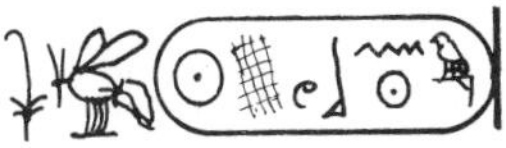

. . . weben Re
Reigned 3 years

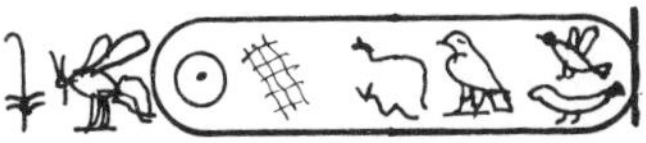

. . . djefa Re
Reigned 4 years

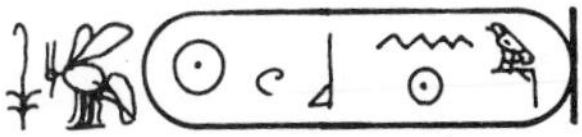

Weben Re

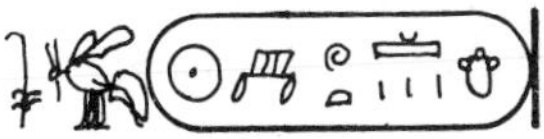

60
67

Au ib Re

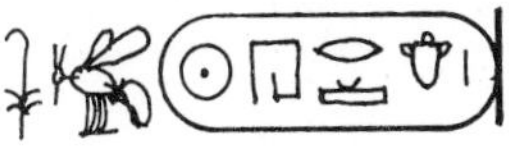

Her ib Re

Neb sen Re

14TH DYNASTY FROM XOIS c 1715-1650 BC

Skheper en Re
Reigned approx 2 yrs

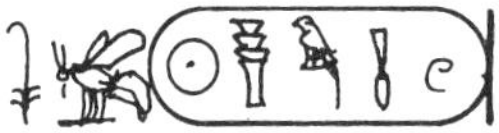

Djed kheru Re
Reigned approx 2½ yrs

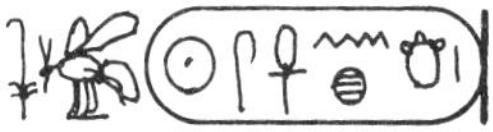

Sankh ib Re

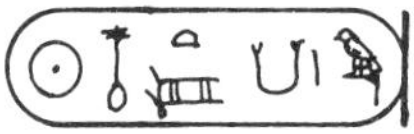

Nefer tem ka Re

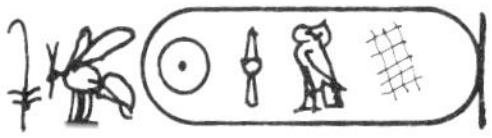

Sekhem . . . Re

Ka kemu Re

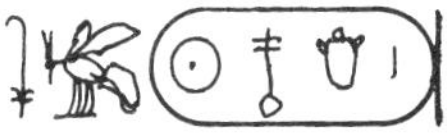

129
145

Nefer ib Re

Ya . . .

Kha . . . Re

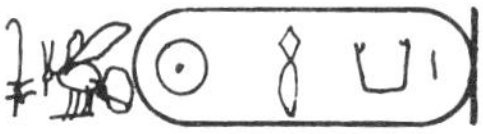

A ka Re

Smen . . . Re

Djed . . . Re

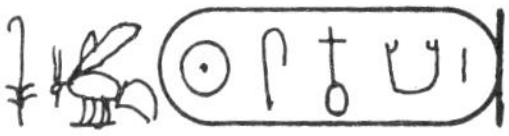

51

Snefer ka Re

128

Men ib Re

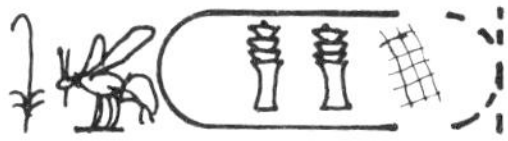

Djed . . .(Re)

76

Ink . . .

14TH DYNASTY FROM XOIS c 1715–1650 BC

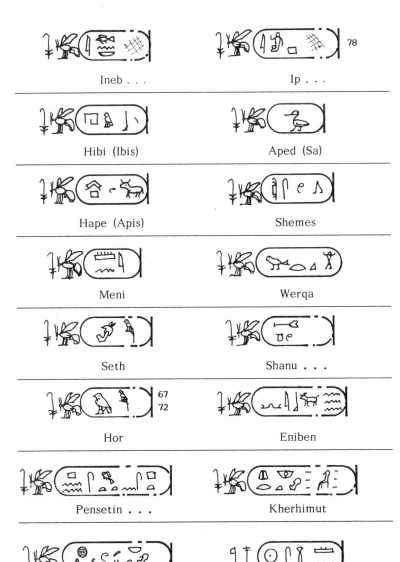

Ineb . . .

78

Ip . . .

Hibi (Ibis)

Aped (Sa)

Hape (Apis)

Shemes

Meni

Werqa

Seth

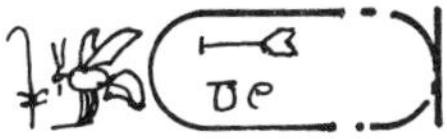

Shanu . . .

67
72

Hor

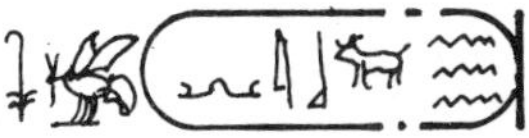

Eniben

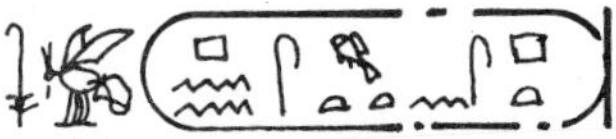

Pensetin . . .

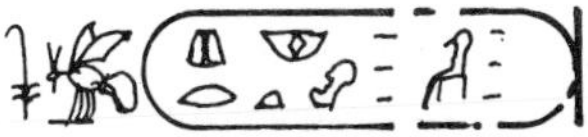

Kherhimut

Khuhim . . .

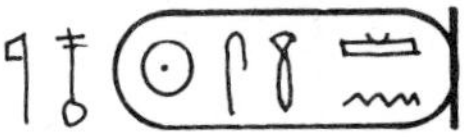

Swadj en Re

SHAREK 15th Dynasty 1652-1636 BC

Sha rek Se kha en Re

The name Sharek comes from the Priest List of Memphis. He is possibly **SAITES (SALITIS)**, M, the first of 6 kings from Phoenicia who seized Memphis. They worshipped the god Sutekh (Set). The two names may be of separate kings.

SAITE (AVARIS)

SHESHI 15th Dynasty 1636-1622 BC

Maat ib Re Sheshi

This king's name was found on scarabs and he is perhaps Manetho's **BNON.** The two names may be of separate kings.

SAITE (AVARIS)

IQUEBHER 15th Dynasty 1622-1614 BC

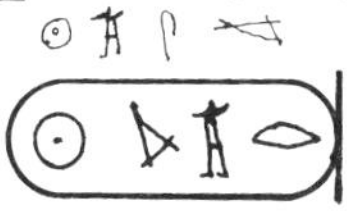

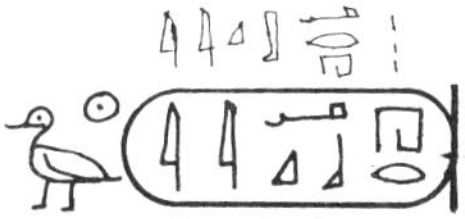

Mer user Re Iqueb her

Possibly the third Hyksos king of Manetho's list - **PACHNAN (APACHNAN).** Name found on scarabs.

SAITE (AVARIS)

KHIAN 15th Dynasty 1614-1594 BC

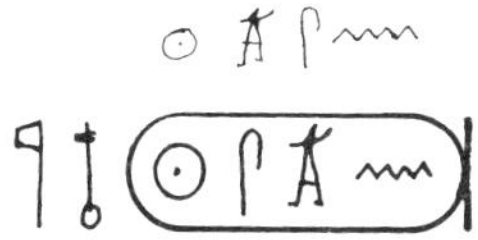

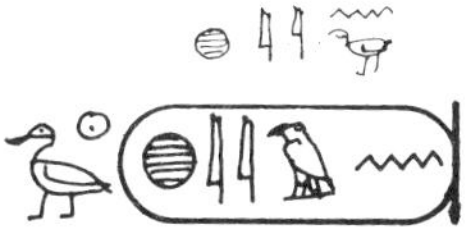

Se user en Re Khian

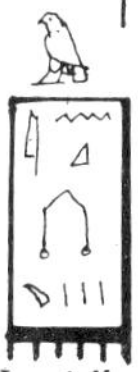

Inqidbu

This king may be Manetho's **STAAN (IANNAS)**, his name is found on scarabs, cylinder seals, an alabaster bowl and a small lion, etc. His Horus name means 'Embracer of the Two Lands'.

SAITE

APOPI I 15th Dynasty c 1594 BC

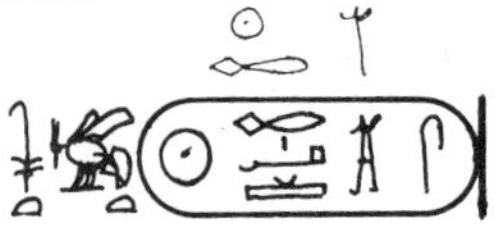  47

A user Re Apopi (Apepi)

Probably Manetho's **APHOPHIS.** Various items from Bubastis record his name. Although a Hyksos king, he called himself 'Son of Re'. The Rhind Mathematical Papyrus dates from his reign. He seems to have had a wide influence throughout Egypt.

Sehotep . . . SAITE (AVARIS)

APOPI II 15th Dynasty c 1594 BC

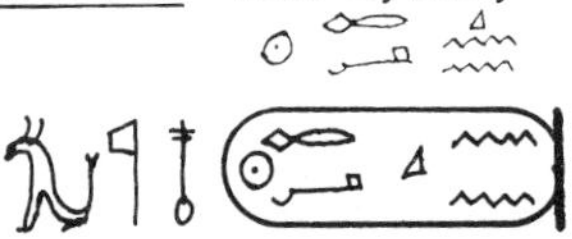 

A ken en Re Apopi (Apepi)

He had his name inscribed on the black granite statues of King Mermashau (Temple of Tanis). Names also found on a table of offerings to Set (Memphis). Manetho only records one Aphophis, so perhaps this king, the King Auserre, and the next King Nebkhepeshre, are the same.

Sehoteptowe SAITE (AVARIS)

APOPI III 15th Dynasty c 1594 BC

  47

Neb khepesh Re Apopi (Apepi)

This king is known only from a few items: a bronze dagger from a tomb at Saqqara, a fragment of silex, and some scarabs. He may possibly be Manetho's **APHOPHIS,** see the above king.

SAITE (AVARIS)

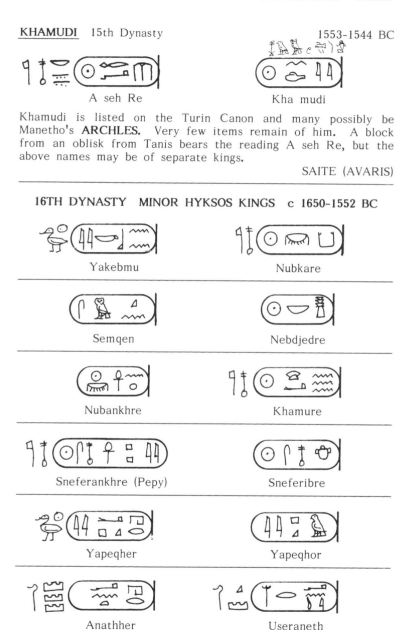

KHAMUDI 15th Dynasty 1553-1544 BC

A seh Re

Kha mudi

Khamudi is listed on the Turin Canon and many possibly be Manetho's **ARCHLES.** Very few items remain of him. A block from an oblisk from Tanis bears the reading A seh Re, but the above names may be of separate kings.

SAITE (AVARIS)

16TH DYNASTY MINOR HYKSOS KINGS c 1650-1552 BC

Yakebmu

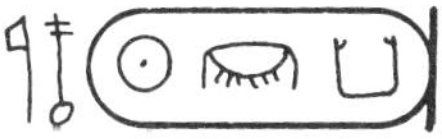

Nubkare

Semqen

Nebdjedre

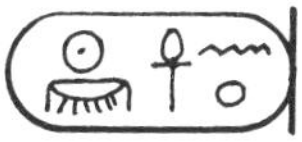

Nubankhre

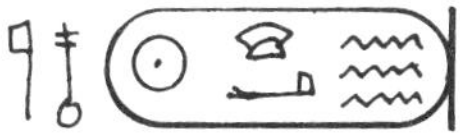

Khamure

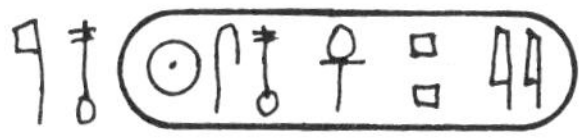

Sneferankhre (Pepy)

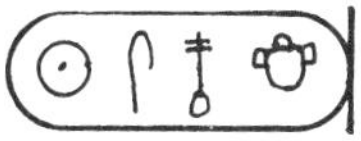

Sneferibre

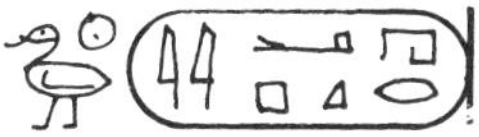

Yapeqher

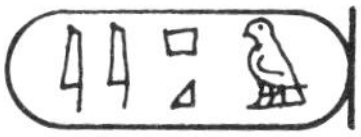

Yapeqhor

Anathher

Useraneth

16TH DYNASTY MINOR HYKSOS KINGS c 1650-1552 BC

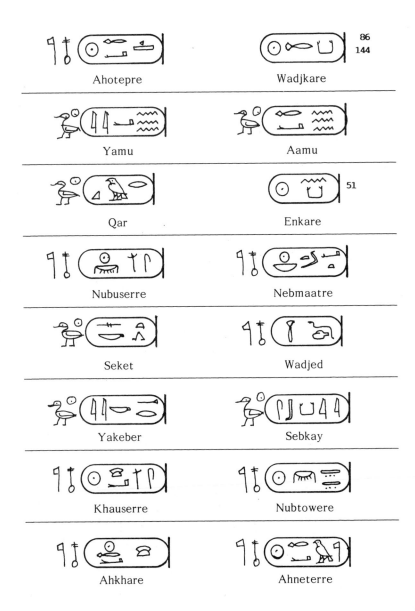

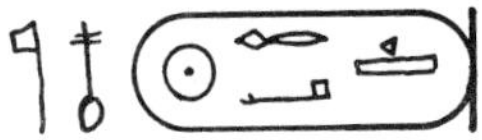

Ahotepre

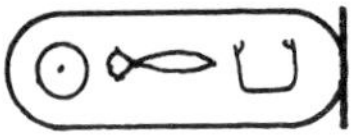

86
144

Wadjkare

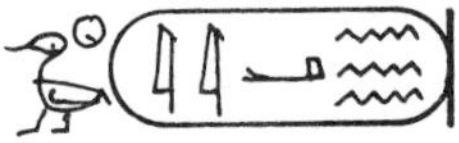

Yamu

Aamu

Qar

51

Enkare

Nubuserre

Nebmaatre

Seket

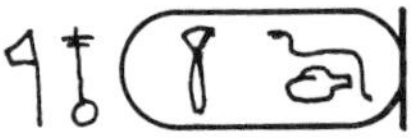

Wadjed

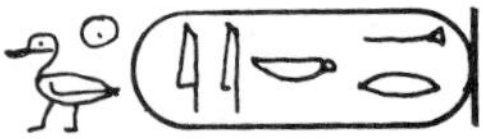

Yakeber

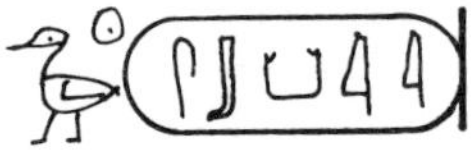

Sebkay

Khauserre

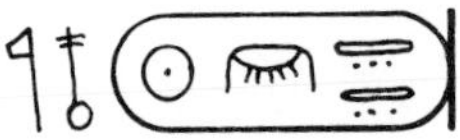

Nubtowere

Ahkhare

Ahneterre

INYOTEF V 17th Dynasty 1652-1647 BC

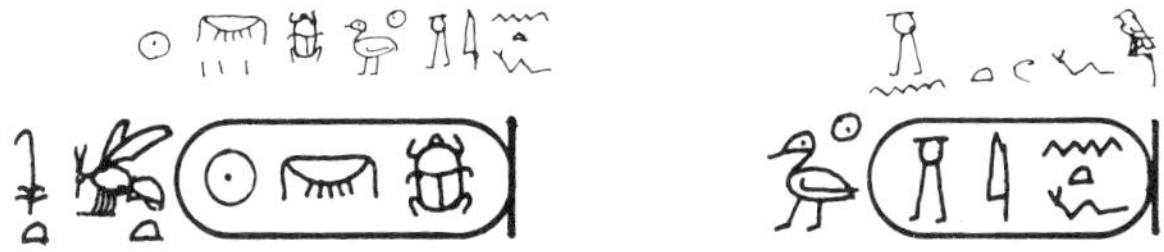

68
84

Nub kheper Re In yotef

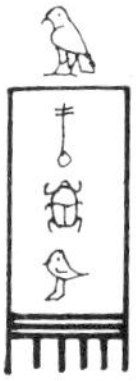

This king's pyramid tomb at Thebes is mentioned on the Abbot Papyrus as being inspected in the time of Ramesses IX because of tomb robbers. His lineage is not clear but he may have belonged to the line of Nebhepetre (12th Dynasty), as he used it as his Golden Horus name. His coffin is now in the British Museum.

Neferkheperu THEBES

REHOTEP 17th Dynasty 1647-1644 BC

Sekhem Re-wah khau Re hotep

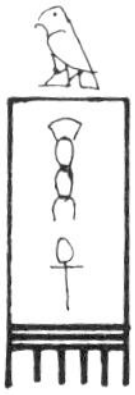

Very little is known about this king, only a few items have survived - a stele from the Temple of Koptos mentions him with Queen Sobekemsaf, perhaps his mother. A stele of Setankhptah from Abydos, also bears his name. Some scarabs and ostraca also. This king's name is found on the Turin Canon and the Karnak List.

Wahankh THEBES

SEBEKEMSAF I 17th Dynasty 1644-1628 BC

84

Sekhem Re-wadj khau Sebek em sa f

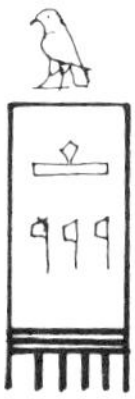

Little is known of this king but his name is well recorded. He is on the Turin and Karnak lists and a small oblisk of his was found in a cache of statues at Karnak. An inscription in the Wadi Hammamat bears his name and numerous small items of his have been found. His Son of Re name means 'Sobek is his Protector'.

Hotepneferu THEBES

DHUTI 17th Dynasty — 1628-1627 BC

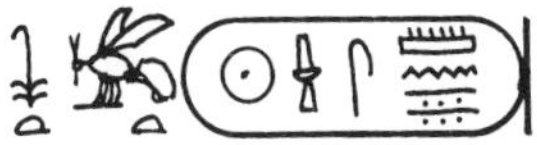

Sekhem Re-smen towe

Dhuti

This king reigned 1 year according to the Turin Canon, and is also named on the Karnak List. A canopic box of his, re-worked as a toiletry box for his Queen Mentuhotep, was found in her tomb at Thebes. None of his funerary items have been found and he is not mentioned in ancient lists of the tomb inspectors.

THEBES

MENTUHOTEP VI 17th Dynasty — 1627-1626 BC

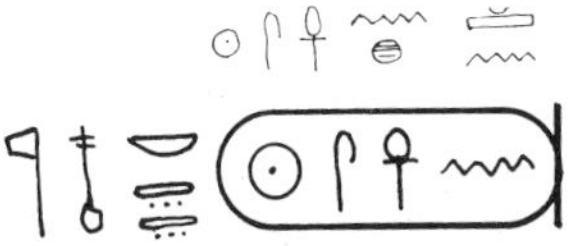

Se ankh en Re

71
87

Mentu hotep

Seankhenre is placed by the Turin Canon, but few items have survived. The two names are linked only from fragments of a dedication to Horus of Edfu, found at Edfu. The name on the Turin Canon might however, be read Sewadjenre, (but see below), thus making Mentuhotep a different king.

THEBES

NEBIRIAURE I 17th Dynasty — 1626-1607 BC

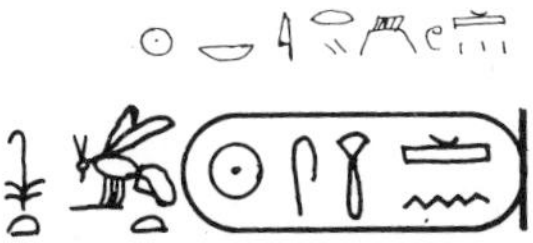

86

Se wadj en Re

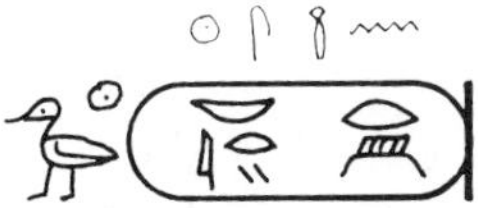

Neb iri au Re

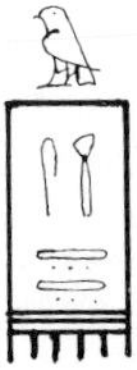

Sewadjtowe

Well known from a stele from Karnak (over a debt of 60 Debend gold), dealing with legal proceedings incurred by the Mayor of the town of el-Kab. A few other items have been found with his name on:- a bronze dagger, scarabs, statues, and he is listed on both the Turin Canon and the Karnak List.

THEBES

NEBIRIAURE II 17th Dynasty c 1607 BC

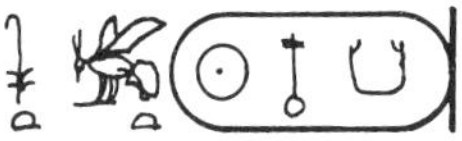

52
118

Nefer ka Re Neb iri au Re

Inscriptions on the Osiris sarcophagus from the tomb of the Horus Djer in Abydos, give the two names. The Son of Re name being a shortened version of that given by the Turin Canon. Name also on a few statuettes, but otherwise nothing much is known of him.

Djedkheperu THEBES

SMENENRE 17th Dynasty 1607-1606 BC

Semen en Re

This king is known only from the Turin Canon, placed between Nebiriaure II and the following King Seuserenre. Otherwise nothing is known of him. His reign, obliterated on the Turin Canon, must have been short, for nothing seems to have survived. He is not mentioned on the ancient tomb inscription lists.

THEBES

SEUSERENRE 17th Dynasty 1606-1594 BC

Se user en Re

According to the Turin Canon Seuserenre reigned 12 years. The Karnak List gives Userenre. No funerary goods or other relics of his have been found. He is not mentioned on any papyrus referring to tomb inspection or robberies. He thus remains an enigma. Some have identified him with an otherwise unplaced Senwosret.

THEBES

SEBEKEMSAF II 17th Dynasty 1594-1585 BC

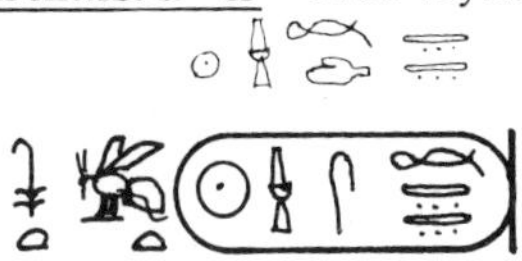

81

Sekhem Re-shed towe Sebek em sa f

Known from the Turin Canon and the Karnak List, this king is also well attested from the monuments. His tomb was broken into by ancient tomb robbers (Papyrus Leopold II), and his mummy and that of his wife Queen Nubkhaes were violated, but the robbers were apprehended and put on trial.

THEBES

INYOTEF VI 17th Dynasty 1585-1580 BC

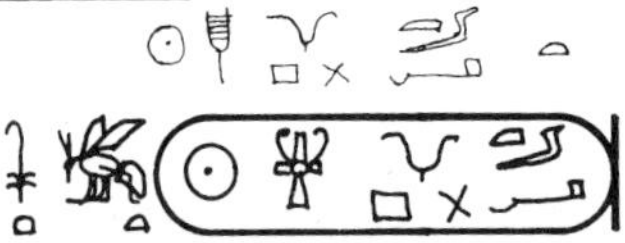

81
86

Sekhem Re-Wep maat In yotef

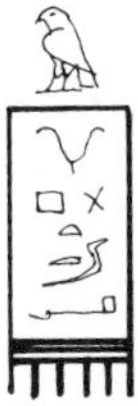

Wepmaat

Not found on the Kings' Lists, but his tomb in the Theban necropolis is mentioned in the Abbot Papyrus as being inspected and found intact. Two coffins from it are now in the Louvre. The one belonging to him was a gift from his brother Sekhemre-herhimaat. The other was Herhimaat's, who must have died soon after.

THEBES

INYOTEF VII 17th Dynasty c 1580 BC

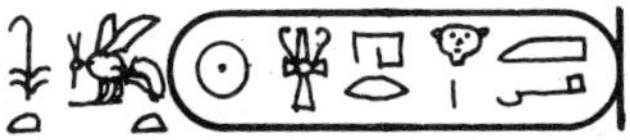

81
86

Sekhem Re-her hi maat In yotef

This king's coffin (now in Louvre), came from the tomb of his older brother Sekhemre-wepmaat. He probably succeeded to the kingship but must have died before long and been hastily buried in his brother's tomb, there being no time to build another tomb. Nothing else is known of him.

THEBES

TA'O I 17th Dynasty 1580-1575 BC

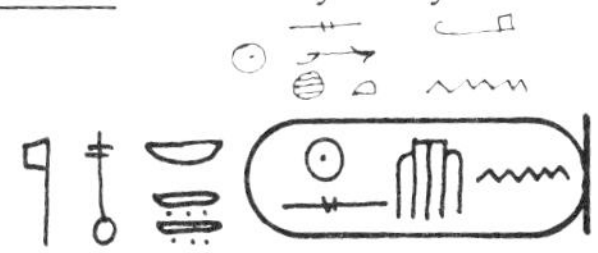

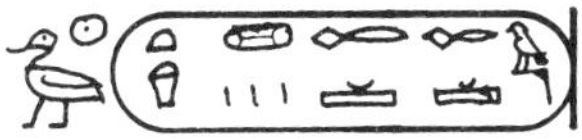

Senakht en Re Ta'o

Little is known of this king but his tomb in the Theban necropolis is mentioned on the tomb inspector's tour as being intact. His name is on a white limestone altar from Thebes alongside the names of the Kings Seqenenre and Kamose, and the Queens Ahhotep and Ahmesnefertari.

THEBES

TA'O II 17th Dynasty 1575-1560 BC

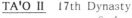

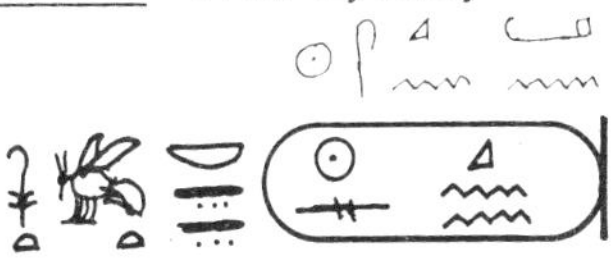

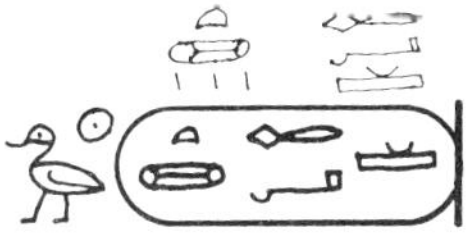

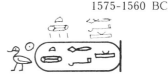

Seqen en Re Ta'o

Under this king the stuggle to expel the Hyksos began. He is referred to in a quarrel with the Hyksos King Apopi, over a noisy hippopotamus at Thebes. His tomb was on the inspector's tour and found to be intact. His mummy was found in the royal cache of Deir el Bahri and it seems that he had died a terrible death in battle.

THEBES

KAMOSE 17th Dynasty 1560-1554 BC

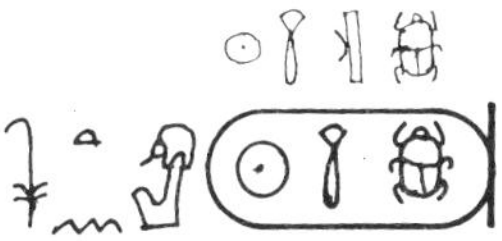

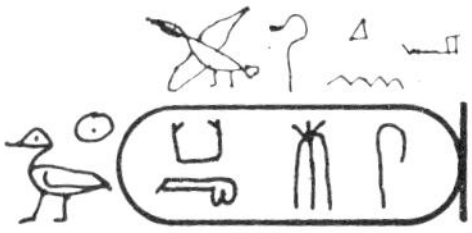

Wadj kheper Re Ka mose

The son of Seqenenre and Queen Ahhotep, he continued the war of liberation against the Hyksos. On a great stele from Karnak, Kamose describes his intention to regain the whole of Egypt from the Hyksos King Auserre Apopi. His tomb at Dra' Abu el-Naga' is mentioned in tomb inspections under Ramesses IX, as being intact.

THEBES

OTHER KINGS NOT IN ORDER OF REIGN BUT PROBABLY BELONGING TO THE THIRD INTERMEDIATE PERIOD

Maat Re - Sebek hotep

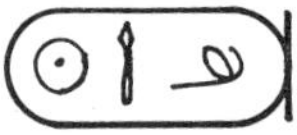

Ah peh Re

Ka set Re

Horus Sekhen

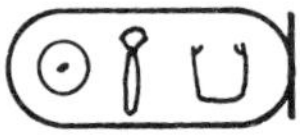

80
144

Wadj ka Re

64
144

Sekhem ka Re

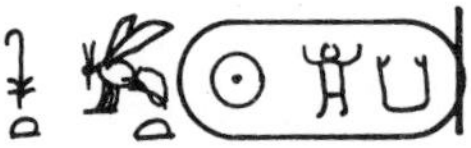

Qa ka Re

81
84

In yotef

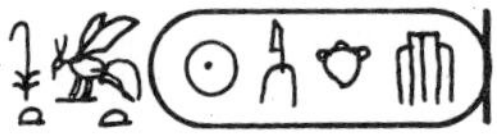

Ib khent Re

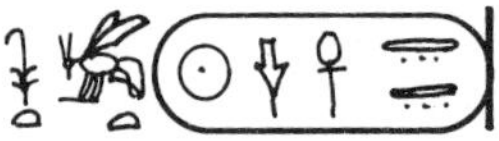

Sekhem Re ankh towe

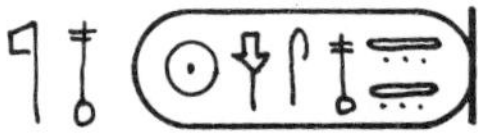

Sekhem Re senefer towe

. . . Set Re

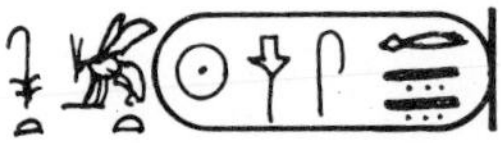

Sekhem Re saa towe

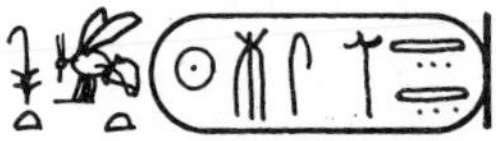

Re mess user towe

82

Se wadj en Re

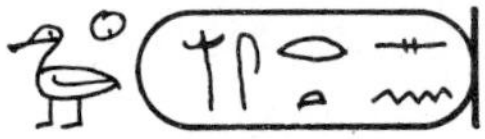

71

Sen wosre

QUEENS, PRINCES AND PRINCESSES OF THIS PERIOD

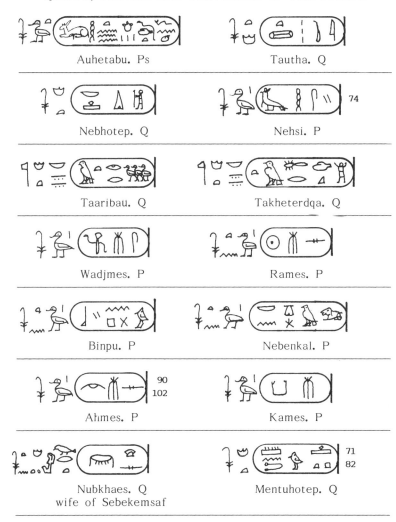

Auhetabu. Ps

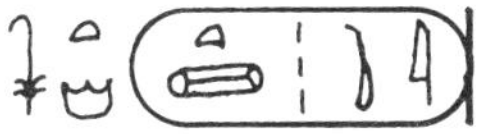

Tautha. Q

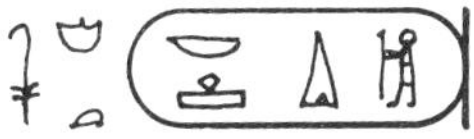

Nebhotep. Q

74

Nehsi. P

Taaribau. Q

Takheterdqa. Q

Wadjmes. P

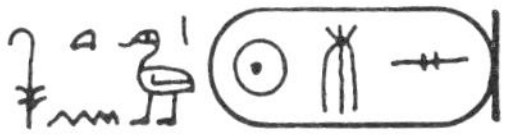

Rames. P

Binpu. P

Nebenkal. P

90
102

Ahmes. P

Kames. P

Nubkhaes. Q
wife of Sebekemsaf

71
82

Mentuhotep. Q

Ahhotep. Q
wife of Teo II

Amosehentempet. Ps
daughter of Q Ahhotep

4.08 REGISTER OF KINGS - NEW KINGDOM
c 1554–1070 BC

18TH DYNASTY 1554-1296 BC (THEBES)

1554	Ahmose	Nebpehtire	90
1529	Amenhotep I	Djeserkare	90
1508	Tuthmosis I	Akheperkare	90
1496	Tuthmosis II	Akheperenre	91
1483	Tuthmosis III	Menkheperre	91
1484	Hatshepsut Q	Maatkare	91
1431	Amenhotep II	Akheperure	92
1405	Tuthmosis IV	Menkheperure	92
1395	Amenhotep III	Nebmaatre	92
1358	Amenhotep IV	Neferkheperure Wahenre	93
1358	Akhenaten	Neferkheperure Wahenre	93
1340	Smenkhkare	Ankhkheperure	93
1338	Tutankhaten	Nebkheperure	94
1338	Tutankhamen	Nebkheperure	94
1328	Ay	Kheperkheperure	95
1324	Horemheb	Djeserkheperure	95

19TH DYNASTY 1296-1190 BC (THEBES)

1296	Ramesses I	Menpehtire	95
1294	Seti I	Menmaatre	96
1279	Ramesses II	Usermaatre setepenre	96
1213	Merenptah	Baenre Hotephirmaat meryamen	96
1203	Seti II	Userkheperure setepenre meryamen	97
1202	Amenmesse	Menmire setepenre	97
1197	Siptah	Akhenre setepenre	97
1192	Tausert Q	Sitre meritamen	98

20TH DYNASTY 1190-1070 BC (THEBES)

1190	Setnakhte	Userkhaure setepenre	98
1188	Ramesses III	Usermaatre meryamen	98
1157	Ramesses IV	Heqamaatre setepenamen	99
1151	Ramesses V	Usermaatre sekheperenre	99
1146	Ramesses VI	Nebmaatre meryamen	99
1138	Ramesses VII	Usermaatre setepenre meryamen	100
1131	Ramesses VIII	Usermaatre akhenamen	100
1126	Ramesses IX	Neferkare setepenre	100
1108	Ramesses X	Khepermaatre setepenre	101
1100	Ramesses XI	Menmaatre setepenptah	101

Ahmose's defeat of the Hyksos freed Egypt from their tyranny and brought its greatest era - the New Kingdom. The Theban family finally dominated. The North and the South were once again united as a mighty empire.

This time the Thebans intended at any cost to hold on to the kingship. The blood line was to be preserved. Co-reigns were set up and brothers married sisters to maintain the line of descent in the 18th Dynasty. In this period Egypt again saw a female Pharaoh, Queen Hatshepsut the daughter of Tuthmosis I. The times were not without their problems however, for the interbreeding may have resulted in the birth of the abnormal King Akhenaten, who abandoned the great God of Thebes Amun (Amen) to install his new sole God of Egypt the Aten. In doing so he also dissolved the power of the high priest of Thebes, which was eventually to cause the downfall of the blood line. Akhenaten and his successors Smenkhkare, Tutankhamen, and Ay, were to be wiped from the Egyptian annals in an attempt to cleanse away his heretical act. Ay's successor Horemheb, the General, fully restored the gods of Egypt, but with him the 18th Dynasty came to a close.

The 19th Dynasty was started by Horemheb's army colleague Ramesses I, a non-royal whose claim to the throne may have been through his wife. Great kings such as Seti I and Ramesses II were born of this line, truly Sons of Re, but the blood line was to fail and the dynasty ended with the second female Pharaoh of the New Kingdom - Queen Tausert.

During the 19th Dynasty the oracle of Amen-Re was used by the priests to confirm their every act. Law and order was by this means vested in their interests.

Setnakhte, of unknown parentage, founded the 20th Dynasty and his son Ramesses III thus began the Ramesside period, which was to prove to be the downfall of the Theban kings.

As the weak Ramesside kings allowed the kingship to deteriorate, the country fell once more into troublesome times. The residence had been moved from Thebes to Pi-Ramesse in the Delta. This allowed the Theban priests to extend their influence and they eventually claimed the throne at Thebes. Egypt was once again divided - Ramesses XI ruling from the Delta, and Herihor ruling from Thebes. Although Ramesses tolerated this situation, the rise of the Theban priests had set the pattern of a divided Egypt which was to eventually deteriorate into chaos. The New Kingdom was over, and no Theban would ever again have uncontested rule over a united Egypt.

The sequence of kings is fairly well known, but some of Manetho's names prove difficult to equate with those from the monuments.

AHMOSE 18th Dynasty 1554-1529 BC

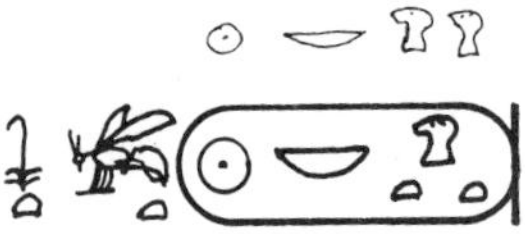

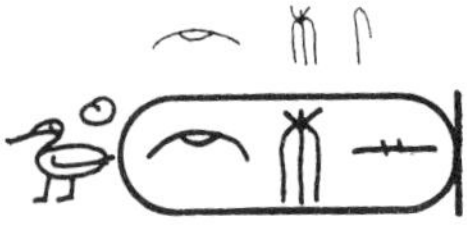

130
87

Neb pehti Re Ah mose

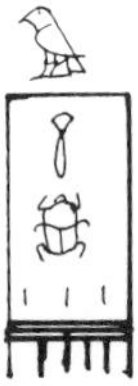

AHMES. AMOSIS. **AMOS**, M. Founded the 18th Dynasty, overthrowing the Hyksos king to re-establish the Theban supremacy. Married his sister Ahmose Nefertari. He was the son of Seqenenre and Queen Ahhotep, and brother of Kamose. Tomb unknown, mummy discovered in the royal cache of Deir el Bahri.

Wadjkheperu THEBES

AMENHOTEP I 18th Dynasty 1529-1508 BC

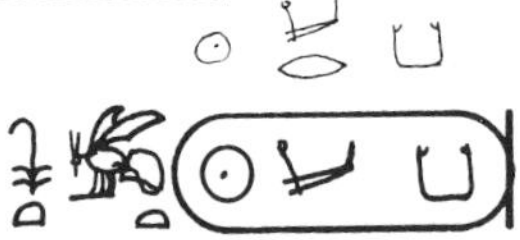

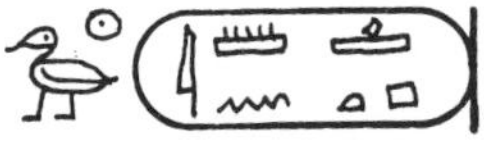

92
93

Djeser ka Re Amen hotep

AMENOPHIS. **AMENOPHTHIS**, M. Son of Amosis and Nefertari, he co-reigned with Nefertari and both were later worshipped as gods. He was a great patron of the priests of Amen-Re. A hillside tomb at Dra' Abu el-Naga' (Carter 1914), was believed to be his. His mummy was discovered in the royal cache of Deir el Bahri.

Kauaf THEBES

TUTHMOSIS I 18th Dynasty 1508-1496 BC

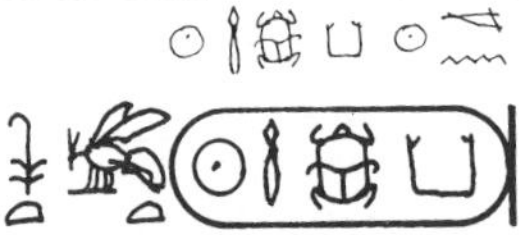

91
92

A kheper ka Re Tuth mosis

TEHUTIMES. THUTMOSE. **TUTHMOSIS**, M. Son of Amenophis I and Queen Senseneb (a non-royal). Married his half-sister Princess Ahmose, daughter of Queen Ahhotep, to secure the throne. Tomb in the Valley of the Kings (Lorett 1898). His mummy was found in the royal cache of Deir el Bahri.

Kanakhtmerymaat THEBES

TUTHMOSIS II 18th Dynasty 1496-1483 BC

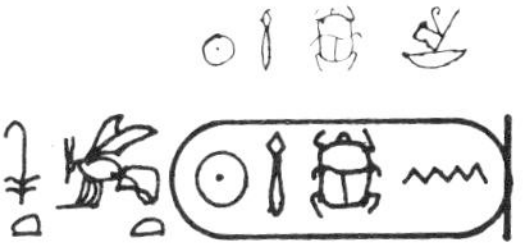

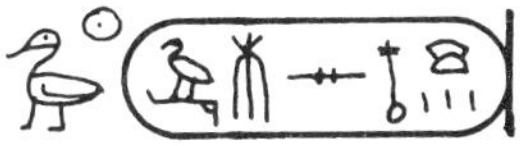

90
92

A kheper en Re Tuth mosis

TEHUTIMES. THUTMOSE. **CHEBROS,** M. Son of Tuthmosis I. Married his half-sister Queen Hatshepsut and co-reigned with her. When he died he left a son Tuthmosis III by another wife, Isis, a non-royal. His tomb has not been found but his mummy was discovered in the royal cache of Deir el Bahri.

Kanakhtuserpehti THEBES

TUTHMOSIS III 18th Dynasty 1483-1429 BC

109
119

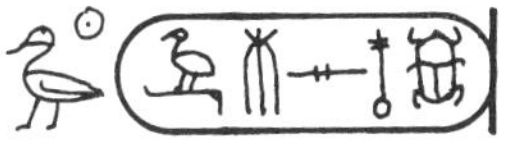

90
92

Men kheper Re Tuth mosis

TEHUTIMES. THUTMOSE. **MISAPHRIS,** M. Son of Tuthmosis II, succeeded his father when aged 9, but Queen Hatshepsut took the throne and ruled all Egypt. He later co-reigned with her then became sole king, presumably upon her death. His tomb is in the Valley of the Kings. Mummy in royal cache of Deir el Bahri.

Kanakhtkhaemuast THEBES

HATSHEPSUT Q 18th Dynasty 1484-1462 BC

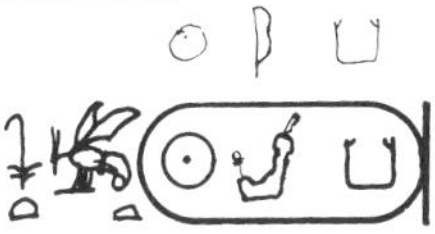

45
122

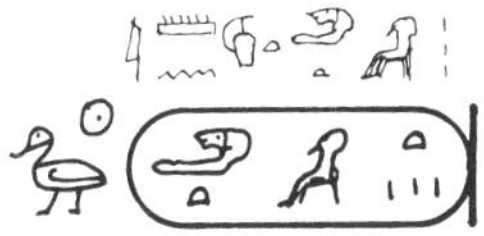

Maat ka Re Hat shep sut

KHNEMT-AMEN. **AMENSIS,** M. Daughter of Tuthmosis I and Queen Ahmose. She may have co-reigned with her father, and her half-brother/husband Tuthmosis II. Seized the throne from her nephew Tuthmosis III and later co-reigned with him. Her tomb is in the Valley of the Kings (Carter 1903) but her mummy has not been found.

Usertkau THEBES

AMENHOTEP II 18th Dynasty 1431-1405 BC

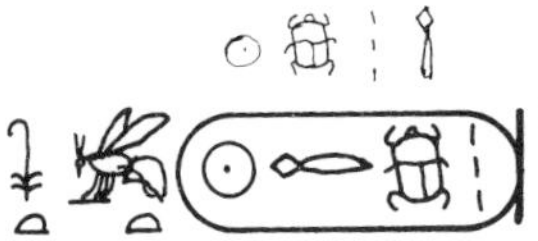

115
145

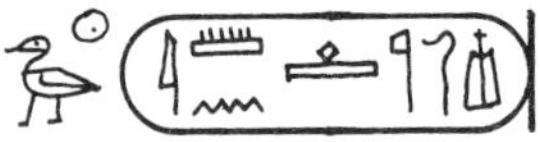

90
93

A kheperu Re — Amen hotep

AMENOPHIS. **MISPHRAGMUTHOSIS,** M. Son of Tuthmosis III. He co-reigned with him for a while before succeeding to the throne. His mother was Meritre the daughter of Queen Hatshepsut. He was renown for his athletic ability. His tomb and mummy were found in the Valley of the Kings (Loret 1898).

Kanakhturpehti THEBES

TUTHMOSIS IV 18th Dynasty 1405-1395 BC

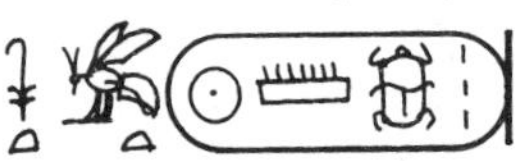

90
91

Men kheperu Re — Tuth mosis

TEHUTIMES. THUTMOSE. **TUTHMOSIS,** M. Son of Amenhotep II and Queen Ta'aa. He was the king of the Dream Stele, which says that the Sphinx promised him the kingship if he would clear away the sand from it. His tomb is in the Valley of the Kings (Carter 1902) and his mummy was found in the tomb of Amenhotep II.

Kanakhttukhau THEBES

AMENHOTEP III 18th Dynasty 1395-1358 BC

146

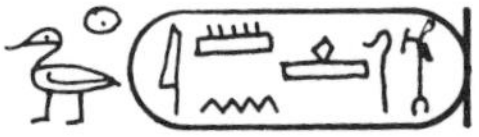

90
93

Neb Maat Re — Amen hotep

AMENOPHIS, M. Son of Tuthmosis IV and Queen Mutemuia. Married to Queen Tiye, whose parents were Yuya and Tuya. Worship of the Aten was favoured during his reign. He built a great temple at Luxor. His tomb is in the West Valley of the Kings (Tolles and De Villes), and his mummy was found in the tomb of Amenhotep II.

Kanakhtkhaemmaat THEBES

AMENHOTEP IV 18th Dynasty 1358-1340 BC

19 90 92

Nefer kheperu Re Wah en Re Amen hotep

ORUS, M. Son of Amenhotep III and Queen Tiye (a non-royal), thus he needed to strengthen the throne and he married Nefertiti, who may have been the daughter of Ay. He adopted the Aten (disk of the sun) as his only god, thus bringing about the notorious religious revolution. See below.

Kanakhtqashuti THEBES

AKHENATEN 18th Dynasty 1358-1340 BC

19

Nefer kheperu Re Wah en Re Akh en Aten

He worshipped the Aten to the exclusion of all other gods, changed his name to Akhenaten and moved the capital from Thebes to Amarna. His reign was accompanied by a dramatic change in art form. The traditional idealised style becoming a realistic personal style. His tomb is at Amarna but his mummy not found.

Kanakhtatenmery THEBES

SMENKHKARE 18th Dynasty 1340-1338 BC

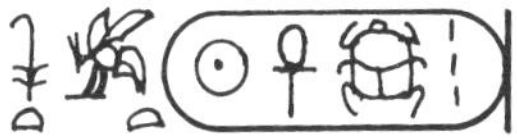

94

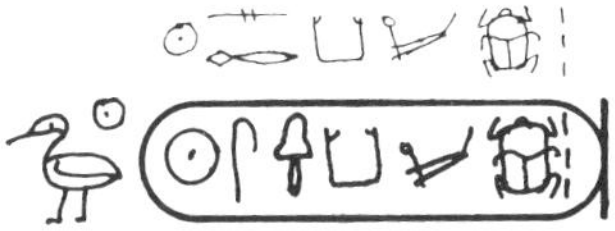

Ankh kheperu Re Smenkh ka Re Djeser kheperu

ACHERRES, M. Perhaps the son of Amenhotep III and Queen Sitamun. Brother of Tutankhaten, he married Meritaten, daughter of Akhenaten who had also been Akhenaten's wife. Meritaten however, died and Smenkhkare then married Ankhesenpaaten, another daughter and wife of Akhenaten. See following page.

THEBES

SMENKHKARE 18th Dynasty 1340-1338 BC

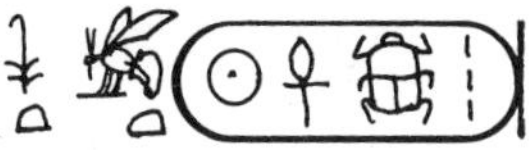

93

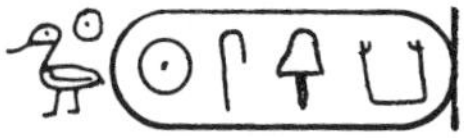

60
93

Ankh kheperu Re Smenkh ka Re

The elder brother of Tutankhaten, he co-reigned with Akhenaten, but then reigned only a short while after Akhenaten's death. His mummy was found in an adulterated coffin in a tomb in the Valley of the Kings, (Davis and Ayrton, 1907). The tomb was thought to be that of Queen Tiye, the non-royal wife of Amenhotep III.

THEBES

TUTANKHATEN 18th Dynasty 1338-1328 BC

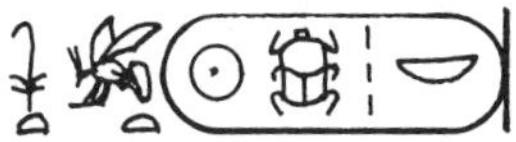

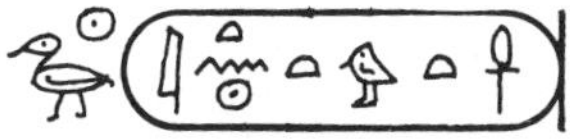

Neb kheperu Re Tut ankh Aten

RATHOS, M. Perhaps the son of Amenhotep III and Queen Sitamun. Brother of Smenkhkare, he married Ankhesenpaaten, the daughter and wife of Akhenaten and the wife of Smenkhkare. Although born a follower of Aten, upon becoming king he renounced Akhenaten's god and restored the Theban God Amen-Re. See below.

Kanakhttutmes

THEBES

TUTANKHAMEN 18th Dynasty 1338-1328 BC

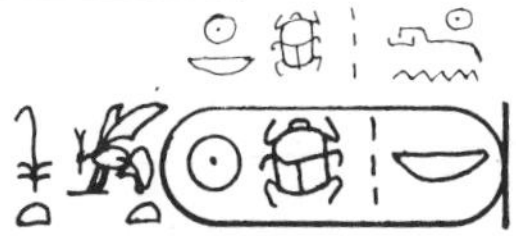

Neb kheperu Re Tut ankh Amen

Upon becoming king he moved the capital from Amarna back to Thebes, changed his name to Tutankhamen (see above), and his wife's to Ankhesenamen. He died at 18 to 20 years of age. His tomb and mummy were found intact in the Valley of the Kings by Howard Carter in 1922.

Kanakhttutmes

THEBES

AY 18th Dynasty 1328-1324 BC

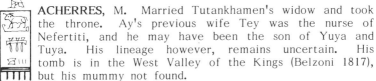

Kheper kheperu Re Ay

ACHERRES, M. Married Tutankhamen's widow and took the throne. Ay's previous wife Tey was the nurse of Nefertiti, and he may have been the son of Yuya and Tuya. His lineage however, remains uncertain. His tomb is in the West Valley of the Kings (Belzoni 1817), but his mummy not found.

Kanakhtthehenkhau THEBES

HOREMHEB 18th Dynasty 1324-1296 BC

Djeser kheperu Re Hor em heb

ARMESIS, M. General of the army and vice-regent of the two lands under Akhenaten. He took the throne after Ay and restored the religion, wiping out the memory of Aten. His wife Mutnefert may have been the sister of Nefertiti. His tomb is in the Valley of the Kings (Davis and Ayrton 1908) but his mummy not found.

Kanakhtsephtsecheru THEBES

RAMESSES I 19th Dynasty 1296-1294 BC

Men pehti Re Ra mess es

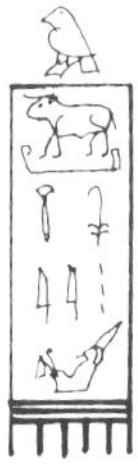

RAMESSES, M. PRA-MESSE an army colleague made vizier by Horemheb, took the throne and became Ramesses I. He was an old man when he succeeded and reigned for a short while only. His tomb is in the Valley of the Kings and his mummy was found in the royal cache of Deir el Bahri.

Kanakhtwadjsutenui THEBES

SETI I 19th Dynasty 1294-1278 BC

Men Maat Re — Seti

SETY. **SETHOS,** M. He promoted the cult of Set (Seth) and restored Egypt's military power. His wife Tui may have been from the line of Akhenaten. He restored the monuments of earlier kings and built a great temple to the gods at Abydos. Tomb in the Valley of the Kings (Belzoni). Mummy in the royal cache of Deir el Bahri.

Kanakhtkhaemuastsankhtowe — THEBES

RAMESSES II 19th Dynasty 1279-1213 BC

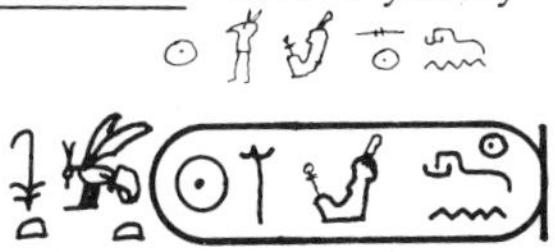

100
114

User Maat Re setepen Re — Ra mess es

RAPSACES, M. Ramesses the Great, son of Seti. A mighty warrior who led the army in numerous conquests. He built the Ramesseum at Thebes and a temple at Abu-Simbel. He had many wives and over 100 children. His tomb is in the Valley of the Kings and his mummy was found in the royal cache of Deir el Bahri.

Kanakhtmerymaat — THEBES

MERENPTAH 19th Dynasty 1213-1203 BC

Ba en Re mery Amen — Mer en Ptah

AMMENEPHTHES, M. Son of Ramesses II by Isinefre. He came to the throne because the heir apparent Prince Amenhirhopshef, son of Nefertari, died before Ramesses II. Merenptah repelled an invasion of Egypt by the Libians. His tomb is in the Valley of the Kings and his mummy was found in the tomb of Amenhotep II (Loret).

Kanakhtaemmaat — THEBES

SETI II 19th Dynasty 1203-1197 BC

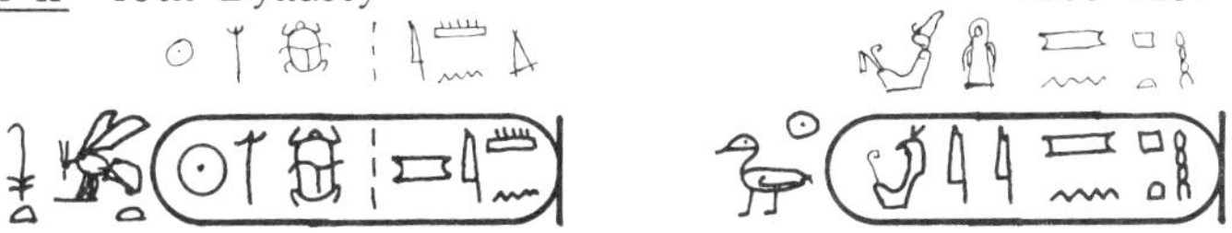

User kheperu Re mery Amen Seti

SETY. **SETHOS** - son of Ammenephthes (Merenptah), whose power lay in chariotry and fleet, M. He built a small temple in the forecourt at Karnak. His chief wife was Tausert. His tomb is in the Valley of the Kings, and his mummy was found in the tomb of Amenhotep II, (Loret 1898).

Kanakhtmeryre THEBES

AMENMESSE 19th Dynasty 1202-1199 BC

Men mi Re setepen Re Amen messe

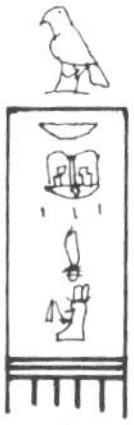

AMMENEMNES, M. Son of Takhare, perhaps a daughter of Ramesses II. He seems to have had no direct right to the kingship, but rather usurped the throne about the time of Seti II's ascension and probably reigned contemporary. His tomb is in the Valley of the Kings, but his mummy has not been found.

Nebsetumerptahtjanen THEBES

SIPTAH 19th Dynasty 1197-1192 BC

Akh en Re setepen Re Si Ptah

MENEPHTES SIPTAHS, M. Son of Seti II, he probably came to the throne by marrying Seti's wife Queen Tausert. He was first named Ramesse-siptah, then changed to Merenptah-siptah. He had a funerary temple at Thebes. Tomb in the Valley of the Kings (Ayrton 1904). Mummy found in tomb of Amenhotep II (Loret).

Khaembit THEBES

TAUSERT Q 19th Dynasty 1192-1190 BC

Sit Re merit Amen Ta usert

TWOSRE. **THUORIS**, M. Chief wife of Seti II, she probably had to accept the youthful Siptah as husband and king. She later took the throne upon his death and became the second female Pharaoh of the New Kingdom. Her tomb is in the Valley of the Kings, but was usurped by Setnakhte. Her mummy has not been found.

THEBES

SETNAKHTE 20th Dynasty 1190-1188 BC

User khau Re setepen Re Set nakhte

SETNEKHTES, M. Parents not known, but he came to the throne an old man and his son Ramesses III co-reigned with him. His name is given on the Harris Papyrus as driving back the Syrians. His tomb in the Valley of the Kings was usurped from Queen Tausert. Coffin found in Amenophis II's tomb, but mummy missing.

Kanakhtwirpehti THEBES

RAMESSES III 20th Dynasty 1188-1157 BC

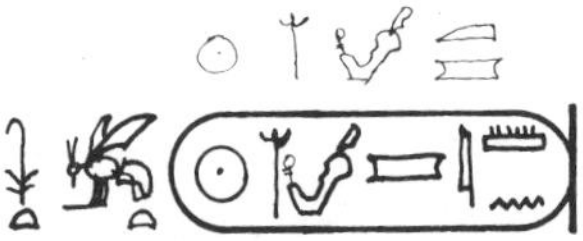

116

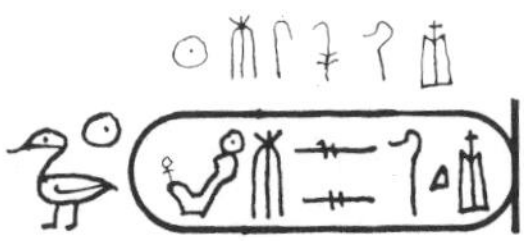

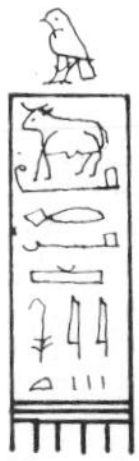

User Maat Re mery Amen Ra mess es

When he ascended the throne Egypt was impoverished. He re-established Egypt's army and navy, and repelled an invasion of Libians. The strike of the tomb workers at Deir el Medina (Thebes) was in his time. His tomb is in the Valley of the Kings. His mummy was found in Queen Nefertari's coffin in the royal cache of Deir el Bahri.

Kanakhtahsutenit THEBES

RAMESSES IV 20th Dynasty 1157-1151 BC

111
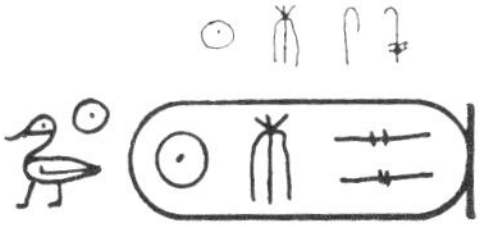

Heqa Maat Re setepen Amen Ra mess es

Son of Ramesses III. He had a peaceful reign. An inscription of his in the Wadi Hammamat quarry states that over 8300 people were required to obtain building blocks for proposed temples. His small tomb in the Valley of the Kings contained a huge sarcophagus but his mummy was found in the tomb of Amenhotep II (Loret).

Kanakhtankhenmaat THEBES

RAMESSES V 20th Dynasty 1151-1138 BC

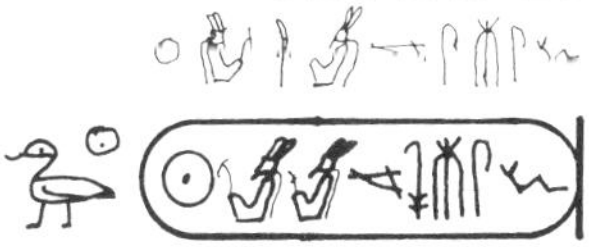

User Maat Re se kheper en Re Ra mess es

Thought to be a usurper of the throne, he may have been the brother of Ramesses IV, but not next in line as he was disposed by the rightful heir his brother Ramesses VI, who also usurped his tomb in the Valley of the Kings. His mummy was found in the tomb of Amenhotep II (Loret 1898). He died of smallpox.

Kanakhtmaatamen THEBES

RAMESSES VI 20th Dynasty 1146-1138 BC

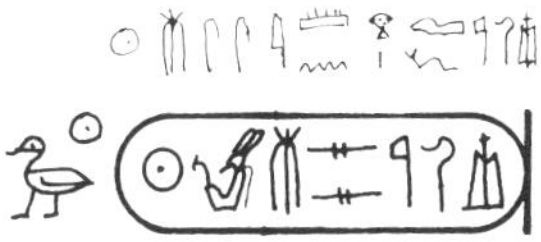
100

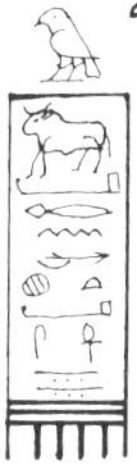

Neb Maat Re mery Amen Ra mess es

Son of Ramesses III. His mother was Isis (Ast). Although the royal residence was now established in the Delta, the kings were still interned at Thebes. His magnificant tomb in the Valley of the Kings was usurped from Rameses V. His mummy was found in the tomb of Amenhotep II (Loret 1898).

Kanakhtahnekhtusankhtowe THEBES

RAMESSES VII 20th Dynasty 1138-1131 BC

96
114

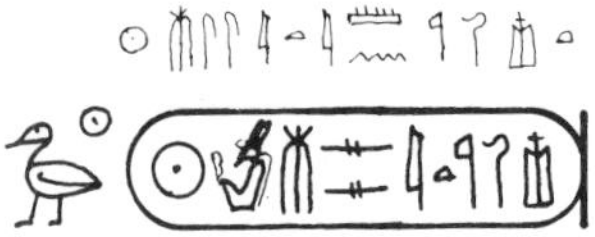

User Maat Re setepen Re — Ra mess es

Son of Ramesses III. Very little is known of this king's reign, which seems to have been insignificant. No major buildings are known from his time, however, he had a tomb built in the Valley of the Kings, although his mummy has not been found.

Kanakhtanemsuten — THEBES

RAMESSES VIII 20th Dynasty 1131-1126 BC

User Maat Re Akh en Amun — Ra mess es

Very little is known about this king, he may have been a son of Ramesses III. His tomb has not been found, but the tomb of crown Prince Montuhirkepeshef in the Valley of the Kings may have been originally made for him. His mummy has not been found. A separate tomb may still lie undiscovered in the Valley of the Kings.

THEBES

RAMESSES IX 20th Dynasty 1126-1108 BC

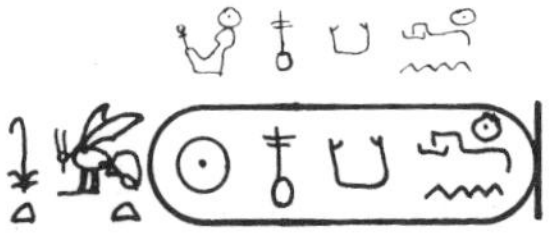

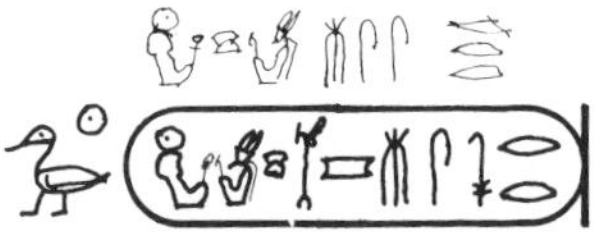

101

Nefer ka Re setepen Re — Ra mess es

He may have been a son of Ramesses III. Ramsacking of the royal tombs at Thebes and prosecution of the tomb robbers, took place in his reign, as recorded in the Abbott, Amherst and Leopold II Papyrus. The robbers were found guilty but their fate is not known. His tomb is in the Valley of the Kings, but his mummy not found.

Kanakhtkhaemuast — THEBES

RAMESSES X 20th Dynasty 1108-1100 BC

Kheper Maat Re setepen Re Ra mess es

There seems to have been a general state of want and unrest during this king's reign, and further tomb robberies took place at Thebes. The power of the high priests at Thebes was growing, the priestly succession had become hereditary. His tomb is in the Valley of the Kings, but his mummy has not been found.

Kanakhtresekhaa THEBES

RAMESSES XI 20th Dynasty 1100-1070 BC

Men Maat Re setepen Ptah Ra mess es

It was during this king's reign that the high priest of Amen, Herihor, became strong enough to claim the kingship of Thebes. Ramesses did not prevent this and thus began the 'Renaissance Era' - the downfall of the New Kingdom. Ramesses' unfinished tomb in the Valley of the Kings was never occupied by him.

Kanakhtmeryre THEBES

HERIHOR 20th Dynasty 1080-1074 BC

During the reign of Ramesses XI, the High Priest of Amen at Thebes was Herihor. He put his name in cartouches and ruled from Thebes. He died before Ramesses and his son Piankhy succeeded him as high priest of Amen. The inauguration of the 'Renaissance Era', ie., 'Repetition of Births', was probably as a result of the growth of the power of the priests. The Priest Kings are dealt with in the next section - the Third Intermediate Period.

QUEENS, PRINCES AND PRINCESSES OF THIS PERIOD
18TH DYNASTY

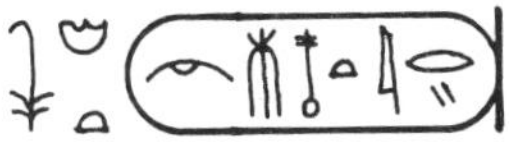

Ahamesnefertari, Q
wife/sister of Ahmose

Ahhotep, Q
wife/sister of Amenhotep

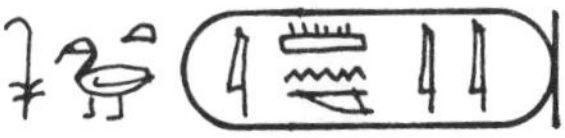

Amenmerit, Ps
daughter of Nefertari

Amensat, Ps
daughter of Nefertari

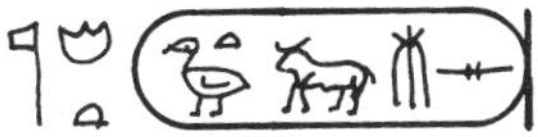

Satkames, Ps
Daughter of Nefertari

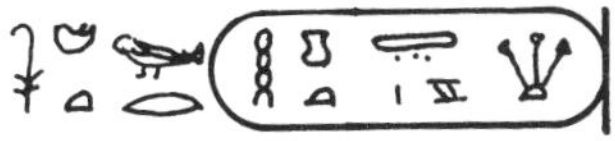

Henttameh, Q
daughter of Ahhotep

Kasmut, Q
wife of Ahmose

Taarn, Ps
daughter of Kasmut

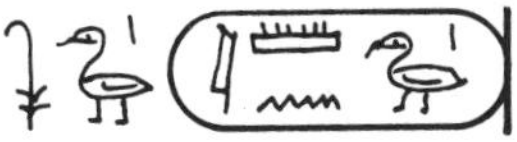

111

Amensa, P
son of Ahmose

Tures, Ps
daughter of Ahmose

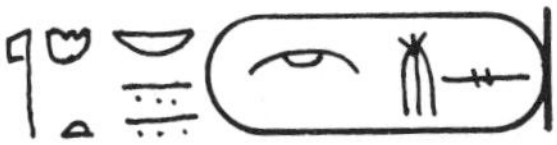

87
90

Ahmes, Ps
daughter of Ahmose

Ahmesnebtowe, Ps

Khebitnefu, Ps
daughter of Tuthmosis I

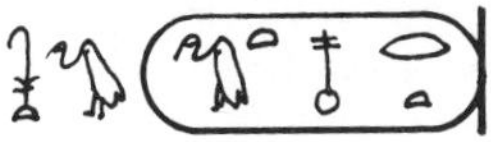

Mutnefert, Q
wife of Tuthmosis I

QUEENS, PRINCES AND PRINCESSES OF THIS PERIOD
18TH DYNASTY

Neferure, Q

Meritre Hatshepsut
wife of Tuthmosis III

Ahsat, Q
wife of Tuthmosis III

Nebtu, Q
wife of Tuthmosis III

Mutemwaa, Q

Arat, Q
c Tuthmosis IV

Tehutimes, P

Ta'aa, Q
mother of Tuthmosis IV

Thi, Q
wife of Amenhotep III

Satamen, Ps
daughter of Amenhotep III

Ast, Ps

Hentemheb, Ps

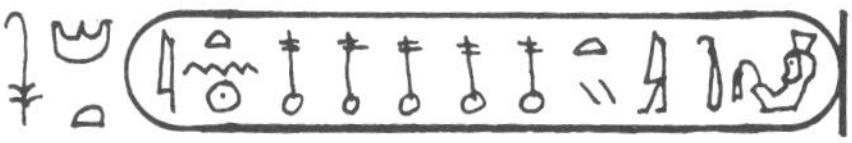

Nefertiti, Q
wife of Amenhotep IV

Nefertiti, Q
wife of Amenhotep IV

QUEENS, PRINCES AND PRINCESSES OF THIS PERIOD

18TH DYNASTY

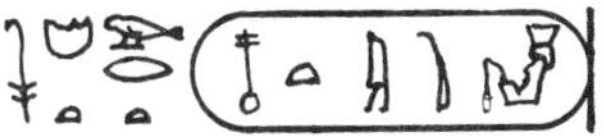

Nefertiti, Q
wife of Amenhotep IV

Henttoweneb, Ps
daughter of Amenhotep III

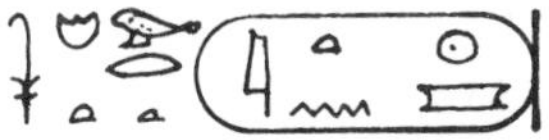

Meritaten, Q
wife of Smenkhkare

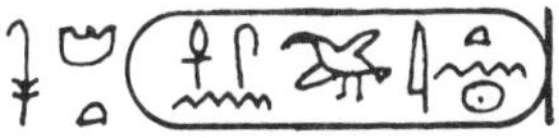

Ankhesenpaaten, Q
wife of Tutankhaten

Ankhesenaten, Q
wife of Tutankhaten

Ankhesenamen, Q
wife of Tutankhamen

Mutnetchemet, Q

Amenmose, P
son of Tuthmosis I

19TH DYNASTY

Nebtowe, Ps
daughter of Ramesses II

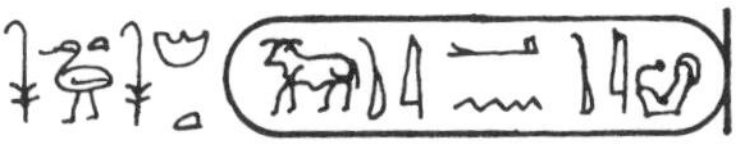

Batauantha, Ps
daughter of Ramesses II

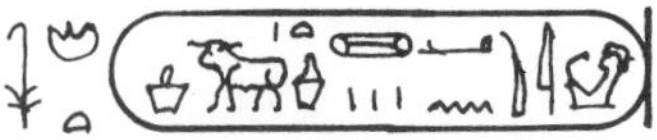

Bentantah, Ps
daughter of Ramesses II

Satre, Q
wife of Ramesses I

Tui, Q
wife of Seti I

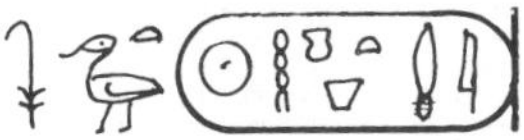

Hentmare, Ps
daughter of Seti I

QUEENS, PRINCES AND PRINCESSES OF THIS PERIOD

19TH DYNASTY

Nefertarimerymut, Q
wife of Ramesses II

Neferumaatre, Q
wife of Ramesses II

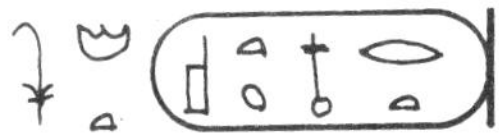

Astnefert, Q
wife of Ramesses II

Sesetsumeryamen, Ps
daughter of Ramesses II

Tummerset, Ps
daughter of Ramesses II

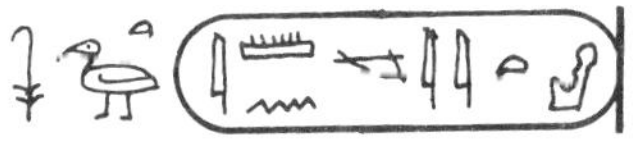

Meritamen, Ps
daughter of Ramesses II

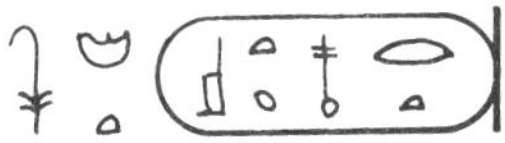

Astnefert, Q
wife of Merenptah

Baketurnre, Q

Thimerenast, Q
wife of Setnakhte

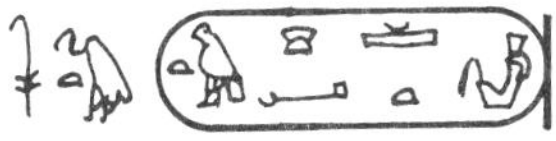

Takhat, Q
Royal Mother

20TH DYNASTY

Astmathruth, Q
wife of Ramesses III

Ast, Q
wife of Ramesses III

Hutmatertchai, Q
wife of Ramesses III

Tuti, Q
wife of Ramesses III

QUEENS, PRINCES AND PRINCESSES OF THIS PERIOD
20TH DYNASTY

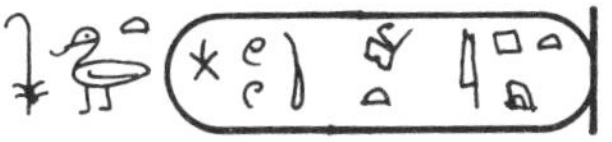

Duatenapet, Ps
daughter of Ramesses IV

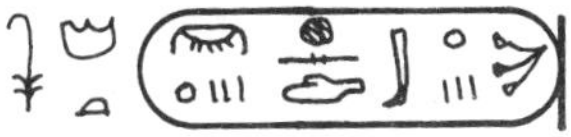

Nubkhesbet, Q
wife of Ramesses VI

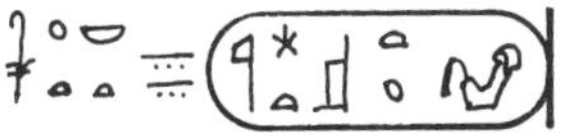

Ast, Ps
daughter of Ramesses VI

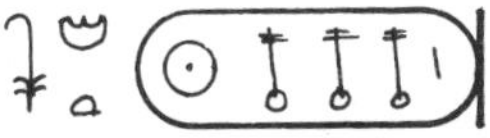

Neferure, Q

Ramesses, P
son of Ramesses III

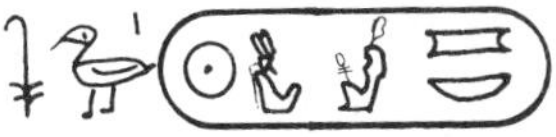

Nebmaatmeryamen, P
son of Ramesses III

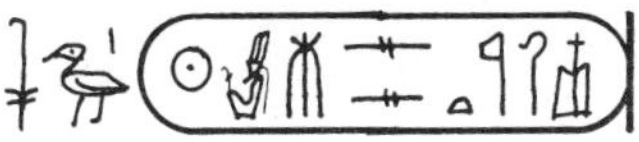

Ramessesamenneter, P
son of Ramesses III

99

Maat Re
Ramesses IV

ALTERNATIVE RAMESSES CARTOUCHES OF THIS PERIOD

100
114

User maat Re setepen Re

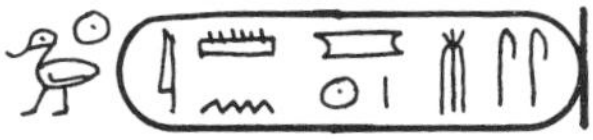

Ramesses II

Neb Maat Re mery Amen

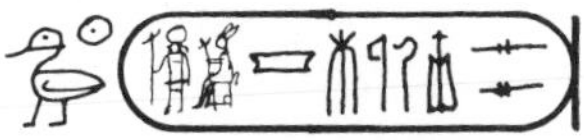

Ramesses VI

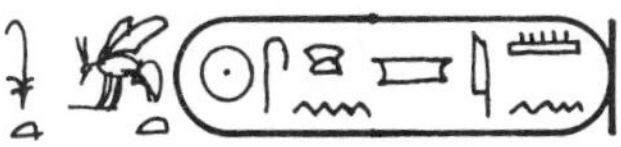

Se kha en Re mery Amen

Ramesses sa Ptah

4.09 REGISTER OF KINGS - THIRD INTERMEDIATE PERIOD

c 1070-715 BC

21ST DYNASTY 1080-945 BC (TANIS)				**21ST DYNASTY** 1080-945 BC HIGH PRIESTS OF THEBES		
1080	Smendes as Governor at Tanis			Herihor	Neterhentepenamen	109
1074				Piankh - High Priest of Amen		
1070	Smendes	Hedjkheperre setepenre	110	Pinudjem I - High Priest of Amen		
1054				Masaharta - High Priest of Amen		
1050				Pinudjem I	Kheperkhare setepenamen	109
1046				Djedkhonsefankh - High Priest of Amen		
1045				Menkheperre - High Priest of Amen		109
1044	Amenemnisu	Neferkare heqwast	110			
1040	Psusennes I	Akheperre setepenamen	110			
993	Amenemope	Usermaatre setepenamen	111			
992				Smendesi II - High Priest of Amen		
990				Pinudjem II - High Priest of Amen		
984	Osochor	Akheperre setepenre	111			
978	Siamun	Neterkheperre setepenamon	111			
969				Psusennes III - High Priest of Amen		
959	Psusennes II (Hor)	Titkheperre setepenamen	112			

22ND DYNASTY 945-715 BC (TANIS-BUBASTIS)				**23RD DYNASTY** 818-725 BC (LEONTOPOLIS-TANIS)		
945	Shoshenq I	Hedjkheperre setepenre	112			
924	Osorkon I	Sekhemkheperre	112			
890	Shoshenq II	Heqakheperre setepenre	113			
889	Takelot I	Usermaatre	113			
874	Osorkon II (Si Bast)	Usermaatre setepenamen	113			
870	Harsiese	Hedjkheperre setepenamen	114			
850	Takelot II (Si Ese)	Hedjkheperre setepenre	114			
825	Shoshenq III	Usermaatre setepenre	114			
818				Pedubast I (Si Bast/Si Ese)	Usermaatre setepenamen	116
804				Iuput I		116
793				Shoshenq IV	Usermaatre meryamen	116
787				Osorkon III (Si Ese)	Usermaatre setepenamen	117
773	Pimay	Usermaatre setepenamen	115			
767	Shoshenq V	Akheperre	115			
764				Takelot III (Si Ese)	Usermaatre setepenamen	117
747	**Probable date of Piankhy's invasion of Egypt to start the 25th Dynasty**					
744				Rudamen	Usermaatre setepenamen	117
741				Iuput II	Usermaatre setepenamen	118
740				Peftjauawybast (HERACLEOPOLIS)	Neferkare	118
730	Osorkon IV	Akheperre setepenamen	115			
728				Nimlot (HERMOPOLIS)		119
720				Shoshenq VI	Wasneterre setepenre	118

24TH DYNASTY 727-695 BC
(SAIS) Contemporary with the end of the 22nd/23rd Dynasty

727	Tefnakht I	Shepsesre	120
720	Bakenrenef	Wahkare	120
715	Ammeris		120

At the death of Ramesses XI, Smendes, Governor at Tanis in the Delta, succeeded but was contested in due course by Pinudjem I, the priest/king at Thebes. In time, as control weakened so imigrants poured into the Delta. Nome leaders became extremely powerful in their own right, and locally supported gods came to prominence.

Tradditional values had suffered under the priestly rule of the Ramesside period. Tomb robberies had become proliferous and corruption had abounded amongst the officials. Great Pharaohs' tombs had been despoiled, but by a quirk of fate this probably saved their mummies for prosperity.

The Pharaohs of the New Kingdom had been buried in all their splendour in the Valley of the Kings, but they were subjected to violation and robbery. The high priests of Thebes were more astute, they secreted away their dead in a safely hidden chamber housing communally a large number of burials, thus forming a priestly cache. In a similar manner they collected the mummies of their Pharaohs and formed another cache. Both caches at Deir el Bahri remained undetected for nearly 3000 years.

A Libian family came to the fore and its leader Shoshenq eventually gained the allegiance of the delta lands and claimed the kingship. He installed his son as high priest at Thebes and thus gained control of all Egypt. The Theban priests driven out, fled to Nubia.

The kings of the Third Intermediate Period followed the traddition of the New Kingdom and honoured the Theban God Amen in their names. Some used the epithet 'Son of Isis', others 'Son of Bast' a delta goddess.

A peaceful period followed with the Bubastite kings having no rivals until, during the reign of Shoshenq III, a chieftain from Sais, Pedubast I, laid claim to the throne. This led the way to chaos, wherein a series of contemporary governor kings from various parts of the country each called himself 'King' and 'Son of Re', and laid claim to the throne. The Bubastite family continued to rule, but their authority was frequently challenged by these governor kings of the 23rd Dynasty. Finally a Nubian king, Kashta, whose authority was probably already recognised down to Thebes, was succeeded by his son Piankhy. Taking advantage of the chaotic state of Lower Egypt Piankhy invaded and conquered, defeating the Bubastite King Osorkon IV and the other contemporary kings, to become sole ruler, establishing the 25th Dynasty and the Nubian rule of Egypt.

Manetho records some of the main kings of this period. For studies on chronology see the work of K A Kitchen and M L Bierbrier (Bibliography).

HERIHOR 21st Dynasty 1080-1074 BC

Neter hentep en Amen Heri hor

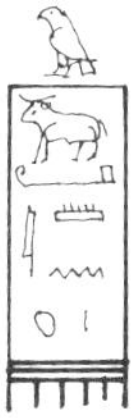

High Priest of Amen under Ramesses XI, he claimed royal titles and governed at Thebes, ruling contemporary with Ramesses. His reign was in the 'Renaissance Era' (Repetition of Births), and probably began the downfall of the New Kingdom. He died before Ramesses and was followed as high priest by his son Piankh. Tomb unknown.

Kanakhtsaamen THEBES

PINUDJEM I 21st Dynasty 1050-1032 BC

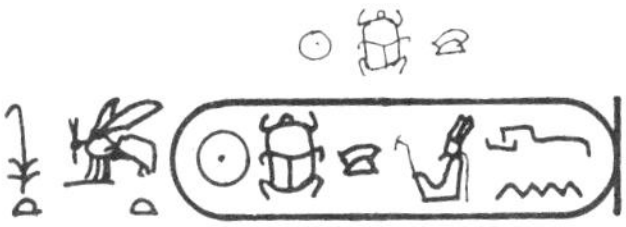

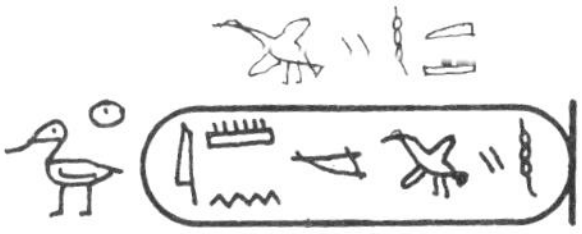

Kheper kha Re setepen Amen Pi nudjem

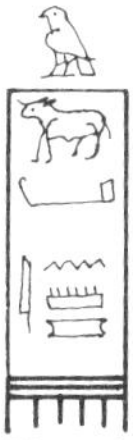

Son of Piankh, son-in-law of King Smendes. He was High Priest of Amen at Thebes. His reign as king was contemporary with Smendes and his successors - Kings Amenemnisu and Psusennes. As high priest he renewed the burials of some of the New Kingdom Pharaohs. He was himself buried at Thebes.

Kanakhtmeryamen THEBES

MENKHEPERRE 21st Dynasty 1045-992 BC

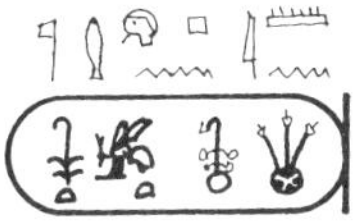

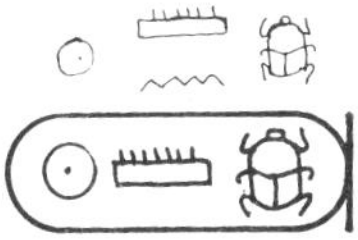

91
119

High Priest of Amen Men kheper Re

Son of Pinudjem I, he was High Priest of Amen at Thebes, following other sons of Pinudjem - Masaharta and Djedkhonsefankh, who probably predeceased him. They didn't claim any royal titles, and Menkheperre's cartouches do not constitute a genuine claim to the throne.

THEBES

SMENDES 21st Dynasty 1070-1044 BC

Hedj kheper Re setepen Re — Nesu ba neb djed

SMENDES, M. Possibly the son of Herihor and Queen Nodjmet, he was Governor of Tanis under Ramesses XI, and succeeded to the throne upon Ramesses' death. When he came to the throne Pinudjem I was High Priest at Thebes. Smendes married Henttowe, a daughter of Ramesses XI. Probably buried at Tanis.

Kanakhtremerysusernakhtamenkepeshferseqamaat — TANIS

AMENEMNISU 21st Dynasty 1044-1040 BC

Nefer ka Re heq Wast — Amen em nisu

NEPHERCHERES, M. In cartouches on items from the tomb of Psusennes I, he was called 'Ruler of Thebes, Beloved of Amen'. Possibly the elder brother of Psusennes and, without an heir apparent, probably co-reigned with him to keep the succession in the family. Manetho put him third in the dynasty, with 4 years reign.

TANIS

PSUSENNES I 21st Dynasty 1040-992 BC

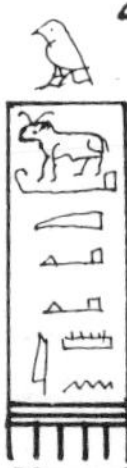

A kheper Re setepen Amen — Psib kha niwt

PSUSENNES, M. May have gained the kingship via his brother Amenemnisu. He was a contemporary of the Theban Priest Kings - Pinudjem I and Menkheperre, and the High Priest of Amen, Masaharta. He usurped the statues and Sphinx of the 12th Dynasty King Amenemhet III. Tomb at Tanis (Montet).

Kanakhtemtataamen — TANIS

AMENEMOPE 21st Dynasty 993-984 BC

113
115

User Maat Re setepen Amen   Amen em ope

AMENOPHTHIS, M. Perhaps the son of Psusennes I, he was king and high priest of Amen at Tanis. His influence at Thebes is attested by evidence from the priest cache of Deir el Bahri. He was interred in an insignificant tomb at Tanis, but was later removed and re-interred in the tomb of Psusennes I.

TANIS

OSOCHOR 21st Dynasty 984-978 BC

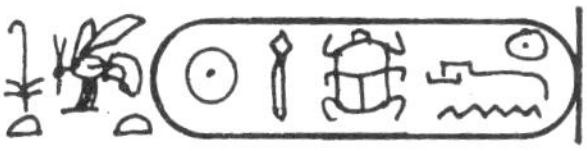

A kheper Re setepen Re

OSOCHOR, M. Other than Manetho's record which allocates him a reign of 6 years, nothing is known of this king. It was probably during his reign that the crown prince of Biban sought refuge in Egypt from King David of Israel. Tomb unknown.

TANIS

SIAMUN 21st Dynasty 978-959 BC

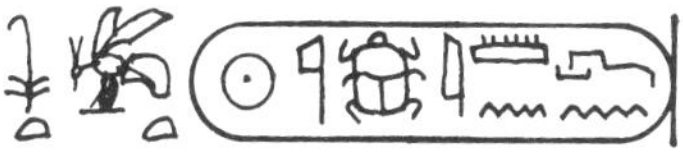

Neter kheper Re setepen Amen   Si Amun

PSINACHES, M. This king's long reign is well attested by monuments and inscriptions. During his reign the new High Priest of Amen, Psusennes III, son of High Priest Pinudjem II, was responsible for collecting the mummies of the New Kingdom Pharaohs and secreting them away in the royal cache of Deir el Bahri.

Kanakhtmerymaat

TANIS

PSUSENNES II 21st Dynasty 959-945 BC

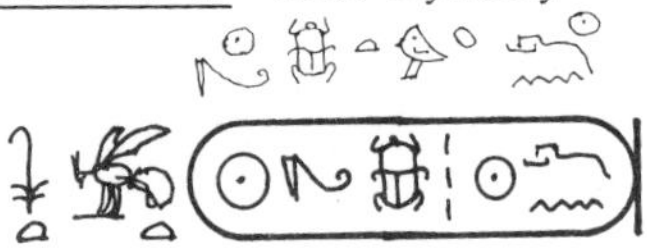

110

Tit kheper Re setepen Amen — Psib kha niwt

PSUSENNES, M. High Priest of Thebes, he succeeded Siamun, who seems to have died without an heir, and became King of Egypt. He was probably of the lineage of King Psusennes I and thus had a claim to the throne. His daughter Maatkare married the Libian Prince Osorkon, son of Shoshenq I. Tomb unknown.

TANIS

SHOSHENQ I 22nd Dynasty 945-924 BC

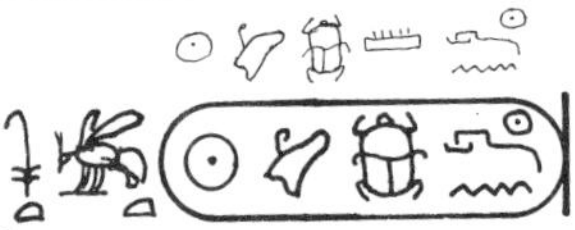
110
114
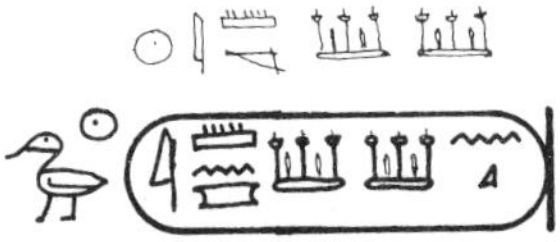
113
114

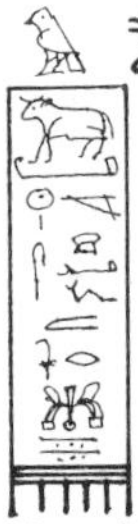

Hedj kheper Re setepen Re — Shosh enq

SESONCHIS, M. He modelled his names on those of King Smendes and tried to unite the two lands. He broke up the monopoly of the Theban priests, appointed his son Iuput as High Priest of Amen and arranged for other members of his court to take leading positions at Thebes.

Kanakhtremerysekherfemsutensamtowe — TANIS-BUBASTIS

OSORKON I 22nd Dynasty 924-889 BC

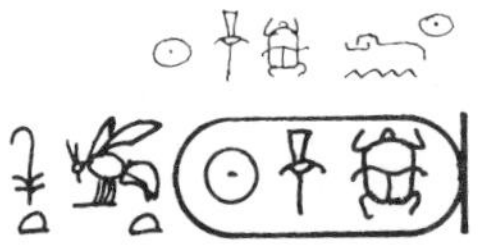
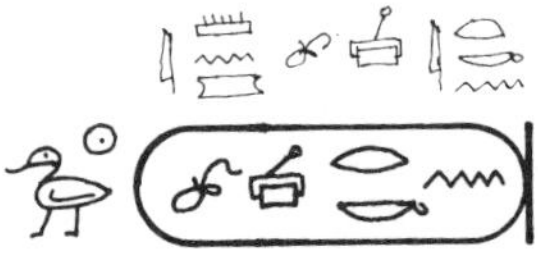
113
115

Sekhem kheper Re — Osor kon

OSORTHON, M. His Horus name was 'Strong Bull, beloved of Re, placed by Atum on the throne to provide for the two lands'. Son of Shoshenq I, he married Maatkare daughter of Psusennes II. His son Shoshenq II co-reigned with him, but predeceased him. When Osorkon died his other son Takelot I came to the throne.

Kanakhtmeryre — TANIS-BUBASTIS

SHOSHENQ II 22nd Dynasty c 890 BC

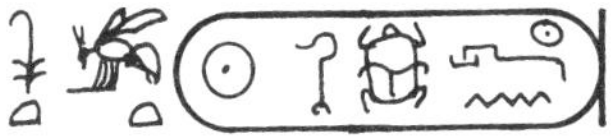

112
114

Heqa kheper Re setepen Re Shosh enq

Probably one of Manetho's 'Three Other Kings'. Son of Osorkon I and Queen Maatkare, he was High Priest of Amen at Thebes, then co-reigned with his father, but died before him. Shoshenq is buried in a side chamber in the tomb of Psusennes I.

TANIS-BUBASTIS

TAKELOT I 22nd Dynasty 889-874 BC

126

114
117

User Maat Re Takelot

Very little is known of this king, he was another son of Osorkon I. His mother was Osorkon's second wife Tashedkhons. His wife Kapes was the mother of his son and successor Osorkon II. His lineage as Takelot is attested by the stele of Pasenhor, but his prenomen User-Maatre is not proven.

TANIS-BUBASTIS

OSORKON II 22nd Dynasty 874-850 BC

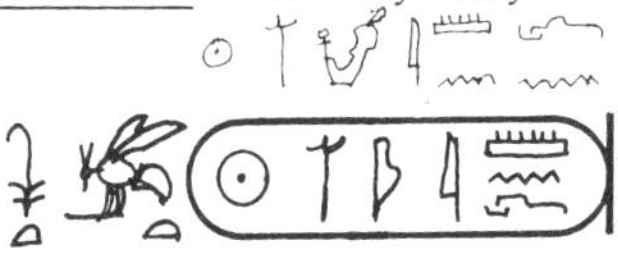

111
115

112
115

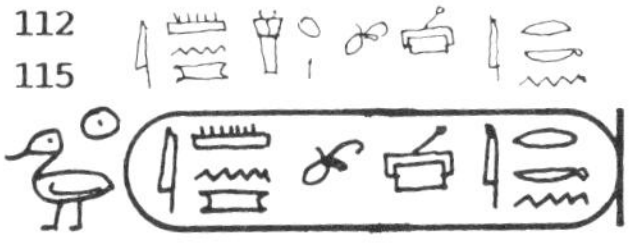

User Maat Re setepen Amen Osor kon

Son of Takelot I. He appointed Harsiese, son of Shoshenq II, as High Priest of Amen at Thebes. This gave the Thebans the opportunity to become strong again which later divided the crown as Harsiese claimed to be king. His heir Prince Shoshenq, High Priest of Ptah predeceased him, so did not become king. Buried at Tanis.

Kanakhtkhaemwast

TANIS-BUBASTIS

HARSIESE 22nd Dynasty 870-860 BC

Hedj kheper Re setepen Amen Har si Ese

Son of Shoshenq II, he was appointed High Priest of Amen at Thebes by King Osorkon II. He was pressed by the Thebans to claim the kingship and ruled jointly with Osorkon II, thus appeasing the militant Thebans. However, he predeceased Osorkon II and was buried in a tomb at Medinet Habu in the Theban necropolis (Holscher).

Kanakhtkhaemwast THEBES

TAKELOT II 22nd Dynasty 850-825 BC

113
117

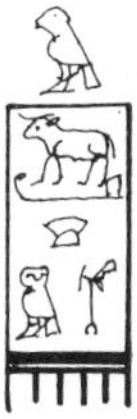

Hedj kheper Re setepen Re Takelot

TAKELOTHIS, M. Son of Osorkon II, he took the throne upon his elder brother Shoshenq's death. His wife Queen Karoma bore him a son Osorkon, heir apparent. Several of his daughters were married off to Theban nobles, thus attempting to strengthen his claim as sole king. He was interred in a chamber within his father's tomb at Tanis.

Kanakhtkhaemwast TANIS-BUBASTIS

SHOSHENQ III 22nd Dynasty 825-773 BC

100
106

113
115

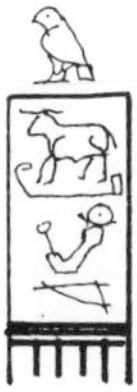

User Maat Re setepen Re Shosh enq

Possibly the son of Takelot II, and younger brother of Prince Osorkon, he may have usurped the throne in his brother's absence. During his 8th year, Pedubast claimed the throne at Tanis, and Egypt was once again under joint rulers. Shoshenq's usurped kingship brought this about. He had a tomb at Tanis (Montet).

Kanakhtmeryre TANIS-BUBASTIS

PIMAY 22nd Dynasty 773-767 BC

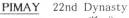

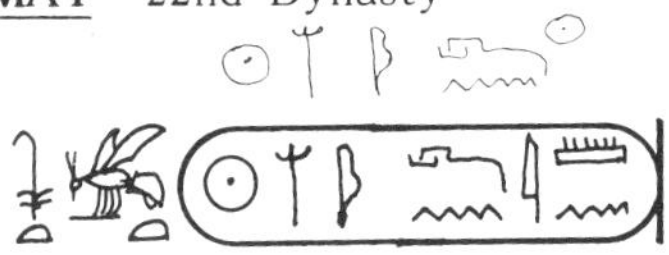
113
116

User Maat Re setepen Amen Pi may

Son of Shoshenq III. Perhaps one of the 'Three Other Kings' mentioned by Manetho. An Apis bull died in his second year and a stele commemorates its death. Otherwise nothing is known of Pimay. The 23rd Dynasty, at Leontopolis, was now being ruled by Osorkon III.

TANIS-BUBASTIS

SHOSHENQ V 22nd Dynasty 767-730 BC

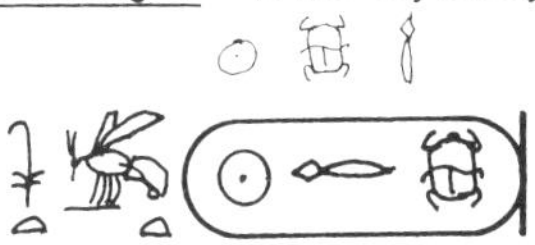

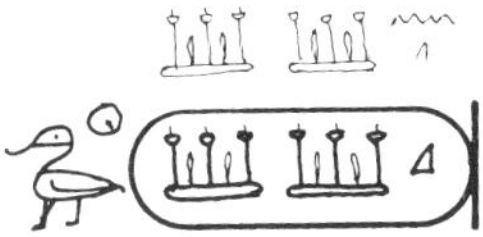
114
116

A kheper Re Shosh enq

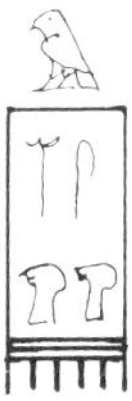

Son of Pimay. Wife Tadibast, heir apparent Osorkon IV. He built a temple at Tanis to the triad of gods, Amen, Mut and Khons. Late in his reign Tefnakht, a Prince of Sais, was waging war and besieged Memphis, eventually controlling more than any of the then ruling kings.

Userpehti

TANIS-BUBASTIS

OSORKON IV 22nd Dynasty 730-715 BC

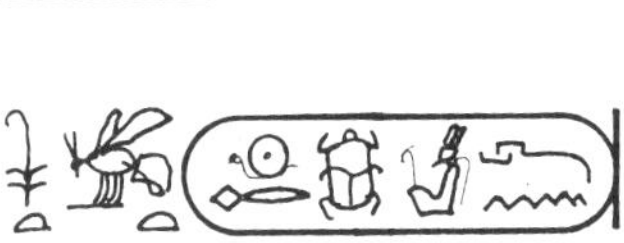
110

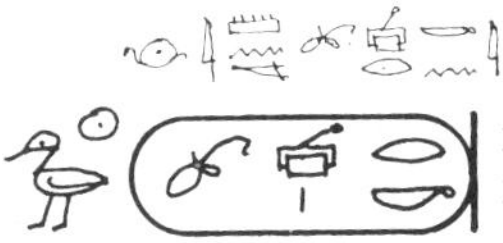
113
117

A kheper Re setepen Amen Osor kon

Following the rise of Prince Tefnakht of the 24th Dynasty, and the death of Shoshenq V, Osorkon IV came to the throne. He was the son of Shoshenq V and Queen Tadibast, and was the last king of the 22nd Dynasty. Although he carried king's titles he was in effect only ruler of Tanis and Bubastis.

TANIS-BUBASTIS

PEDUBAST I 23rd Dynasty 818-793 BC

115 117

121 133

User Maat Re setepen Amen   Pedu Bast

PETUBATES, M. He may have been another son of Takelot II, thus he felt he had a legitimate claim to the throne. He ruled as king at the same time as Shoshenq III, and established a new capital at Leontopolis, to start the 23rd Dynasty. He appointed his son Iuput I as co-regent. Tomb unknown.

LEONTOPOLIS-TANIS

IUPUT I 23rd Dynasty c 804 BC

118

Iu put

Very little is known of this king, he was possibly the son of Pedubast I and he was appointed co-regent in his time. His reign may have been short. During his reign Egypt had co-rulers Shoshenq III, Pedubast I and Iuput I. An indication of the division brought about by the priestly power of the period.

LEONTOPOLIS-TANIS

SHOSHENQ IV 23rd Dynasty 793-787 BC

98

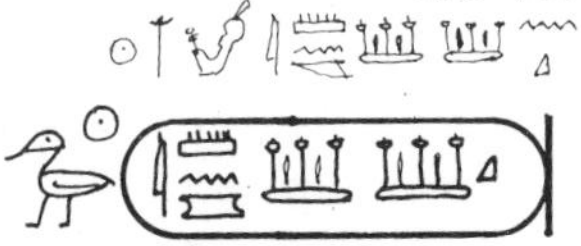

115 118

User Maat Re mery Amen   Shosh enq

He succeeded Iuput I and co-reigned with Pedubast I. Shoshenq III still reigned from Tanis, so Egypt had two different kings with the name of Shoshenq, reigning at the same time. Very little is known of Shoshenq IV. He may have been the son of Iuput I, but this is not confirmed by any monuments.

LEONTOPOLIS-TANIS

OSORKON III 23rd Dynasty 787-759 BC

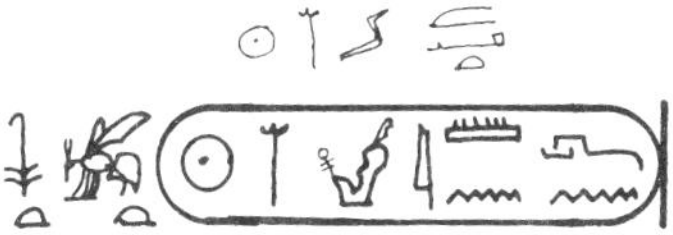

115
118

113
115

User Maat Re setepen Amen — Osor kon

OSORCHO, M. Son of Queen Kamama, his wives were Karoatjet, and Tentsai mother of Takelot III his heir apparent. Another sun Rudamen was also to claim kingly titles. The Theban influence was still strong and in his 24th year he appointed Takelot as High Priest of Amen at Thebes, and then as co-regent.

Kanakhtkhaemwast — LEONTOPOLIS-TANIS

TAKELOT III 23rd Dynasty 764-744 BC

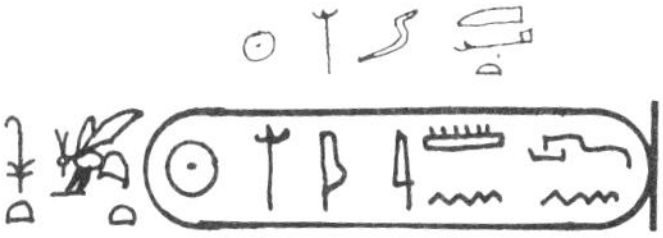

116
118

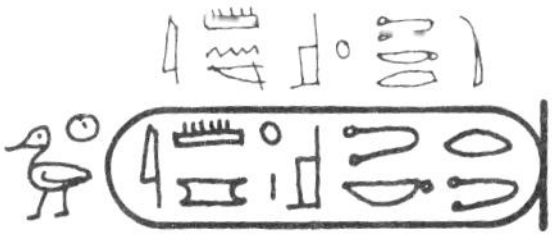

113
114

User Maat Re setepen Amen — Takelot

ZET, M. Son of Osorkon III. When he became co-regent with his father his position as High Priest of Heraclepolis went to Peftjauawybast, who was later to claim kingly titles. Upon his father's death Takelot became sole king, however, other contemporaries ruled - Nimlot at Hermopolis and Shoshenq V at Tanis.

Wadjtowe — LEONTOPOLIS-TANIS

RUDAMEN 23rd Dynasty 744-741 BC

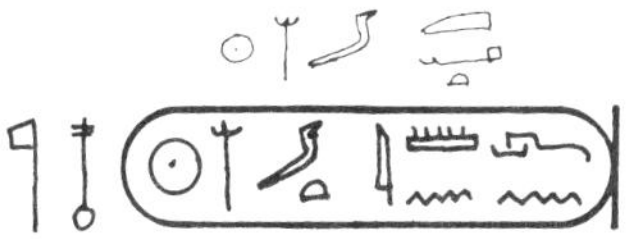

116
118

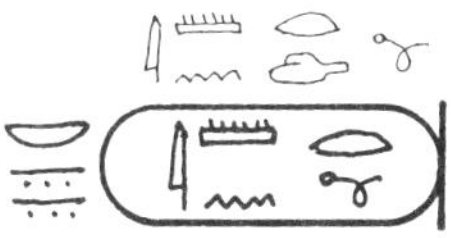

User Maat Re setepen Amen — Rud Amen

Not mentioned by Manetho. He was the younger brother of Takelot III. Married Tadiamun. His son-in-law was Peftjauawybast a king of Heracleopolis. Rudamen's titles were found in a temple of Osiris at Karnak, otherwise very little is known of this king.

Nebmaat — LEONTOPOLIS-TANIS

IUPUT II 23rd Dynasty 741-720 BC

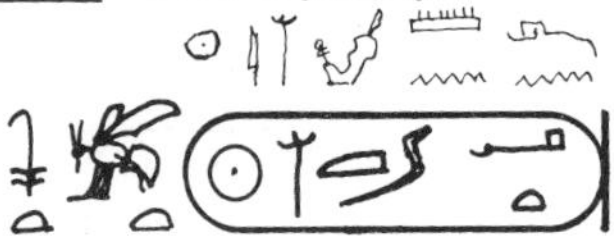
116
117

116

User Maat Re setepen Amen — Iu put

Not mentioned by Manetho. He is mentioned on the stele of the Nubian conqueror Piankhy. Of uncertain lineage, possibly the son of Rudamen he succeeded him, but only ruled locally. Shoshenq V continued to rule at Tanis.

LEONTOPOLIS-TANIS

SHOSHENQ VI 23rd Dynasty 720-715 BC

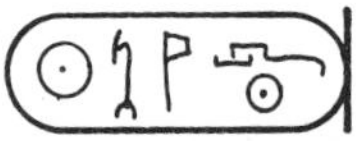

121
116

Was neter Re setepen Re — Shosh enq

Not mentioned by Manetho and very doubtfully attested as a separate king by cartouches on a pendant (Petrie, University College collection), which may be corruptions of those of King Shoshenq III.

LEONTOPOLIS-TANIS

PEFTJAUAWYBAST 23rd Dynasty 740-725 BC

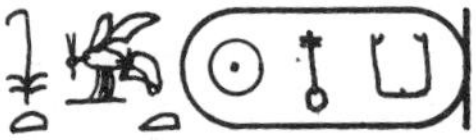
51
126

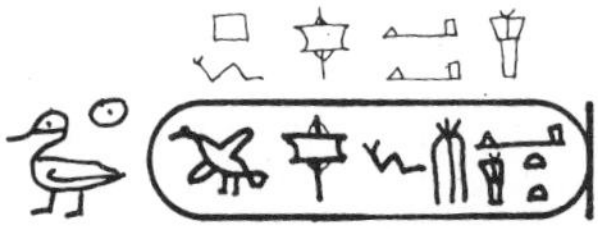

Nefer ka Re — Pef tjau awy Bast

He married Irbastudjanefu, the daughter of King Rudamen of the Leontopolis line of kings. He was initially high priest at Heracleopolis, but took kingly titles and probably ruled only locally. Lineage unknown, but he was appointed High Priest of Heracleopolis at the ascension of Takelot III.

HERACLEOPOLIS

NIMLOT c 23rd Dynasty c 728 BC

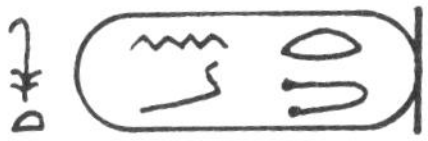

Nim lot

Little is known of this king. Contemporary with Kings - Osorkon IV, Iuput II, Peftjauawybast, and Prince Tefnakht. He was a ruler of Hermopolis at the time of the Nubian invasion and took part in the capitulation of the Egyptian kinglets to Piankhy which began the end of the Third Intermediate Period.

HERMOPOLIS

TUTHEMHET c 23rd/24th Dynasty c 725 BC

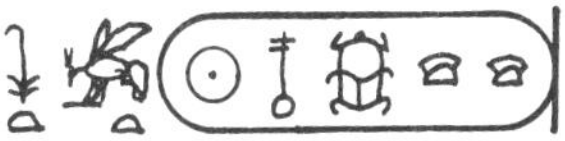

Nefer kheper Re kha kha Tuth em het

Possibly the successor of Nimlot, his names are known only from a few items:- a bronze shrine (British Museum), and a statue from Thebes (Cairo Museum).

Nebatumemmaat

HERMOPOLIS

REMENY c 23rd/24th Dynasty c 720 BC

109
128

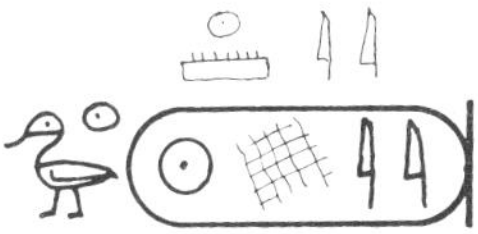

Men kheper Re Re meny

Another local king of the period, known from a stele from Thebes. He used kingly titles but nothing is known of his reign, which was probably during the Nubian period of Thebes. His name is given by some as Khmuny.

Smatowe

HERMOPOLIS

<u>TEFNAKHT I</u> 24th Dynasty 727-720 BC

128

Shepses Re Tef nakht

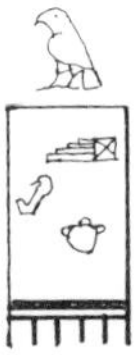

Not mentioned by Manetho, this king was contemporary with Shoshenq V, Osorkon IV and Iuput II. He was a non-royal prince of the West and rose to great power. He was never subservient to Piankhy like the other kings, and when Piankhy returned to Nubia Tefnakht pronounced himself King of the North.

Siaib

SAIS

<u>BAKENRENEF</u> 24th Dynasty 720-715 BC

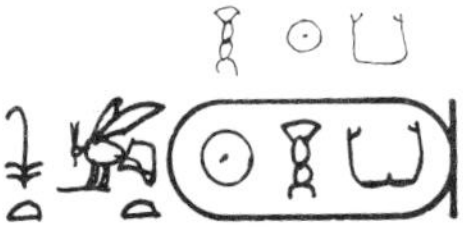

53

Wah ka Re Ba ken ren ef

BOCHCHORIS, M. Possibly the son of Tefnakht, he succeeded his father to rule the North. Meanwhile, Piankhy's successor Shabaka, came North, took Memphis, and defeated Bakenrenef, thus ending the Third Intermediate Period. Manetho claimed that in Bochchoris' time a lamb spoke (and foretold the defeat of Egypt?).

SAIS

<u>AMMERIS</u> 24th Dynasty 715-695 BC

This king is mentioned in Eusebius's version of Manetho as an Ethiopian, but he is not attested by any inscription or monument. He may have been a nominal Nubian Governor installed as ruler of Sais upon the conquest by Shabaka. He is thought by some to have been the Nubian King Tanutamen. This is however, very unlikely as Tanutamen is attested at a later period.

SAIS

OTHER KINGS NOT IN ORDER OF REIGN BUT PROBABLY BELONGING TO THE THIRD INTERMEDIATE PERIOD

SHOSHENQ VII

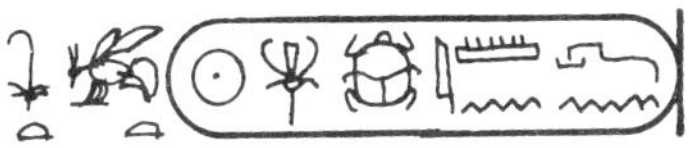
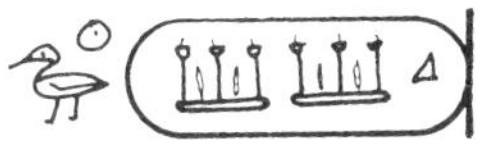

Sekhem kheper Re setepen Amen — Shosh enq

The cartouches of this king as a separate ruler, are very doubtfully attested. They are found on a stele from Florence, and on a scarab. They may be variants of the names of King Osorkon I.

GEMENEFKHONSBAK

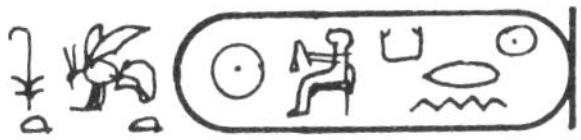

Shepses ka Re Iren Re — Gemen ef Khons Bak

This king is unknown, other than his cartouche from the Delta. He was very likely a local governor/king of Tanis.

PEDUBAST II

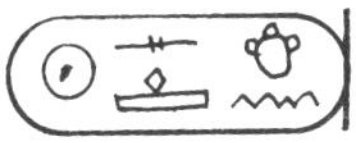
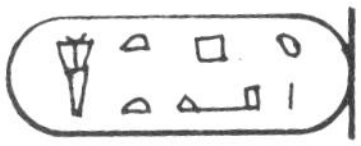
133

Sehotep ib en Re — Pedu Bast

Little is known of this king, but his name was found on blocks from Tanis. His position in this period is not attested.

. . . MERYTOWEPENAMEN

. . . mery towe Pen Amen

This king's cartouche was found on a block from Tanis, but his position in this period is not attested. He may be of a later period. Otherwise nothing is known of him.

QUEENS, PRINCESSES AND GOD'S WIVES OF THIS PERIOD

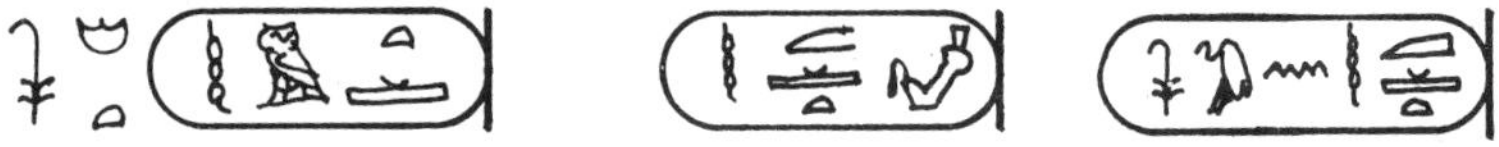

Nodjmet, Q - wife of Herihor

Tentamen, Q - wife of Smendes

Henttowe - Princess, God's Wife, Queen, various - daughter of Smendes, wife of Pinudjem I and mother of Psusennes I.

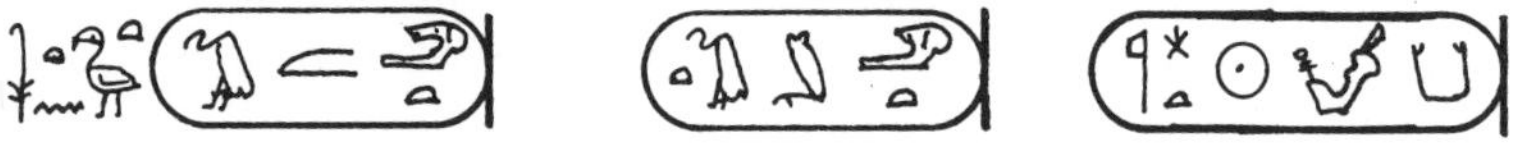

Mutemhet High Priestess Maatkare

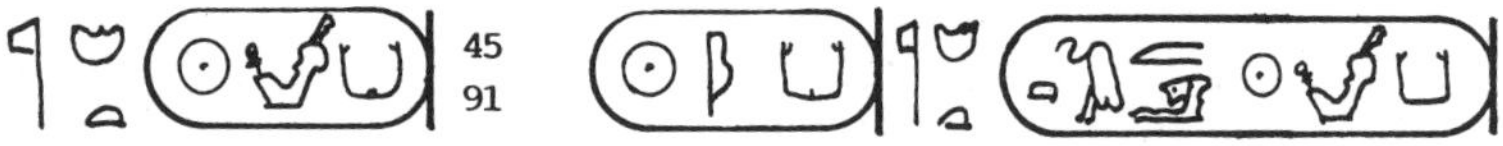

Titles of Maatkare - daughter of Pinudjem I

Istemkheb God's Wife of Amen

Daughter of Psusennes I

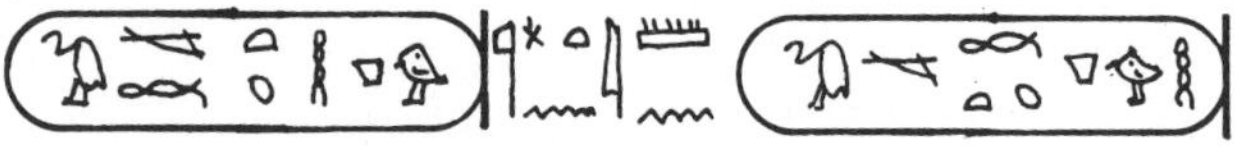

Mehtenweskhetmerymut

Grandmother of Shoshenq I

QUEENS, PRINCESSES AND GOD'S WIVES OF THIS PERIOD

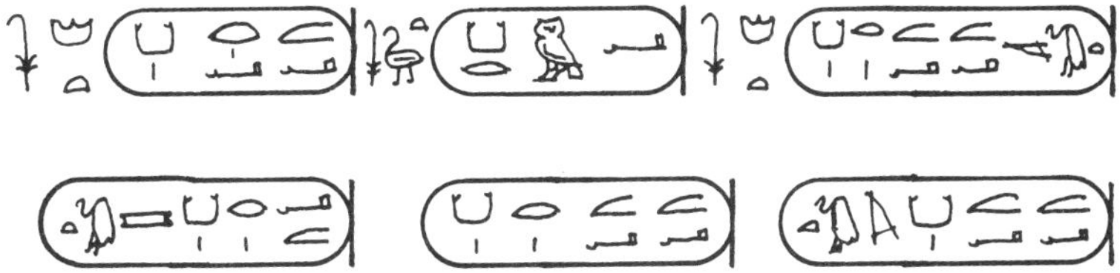

Various - Karama(t) - Karamama - Kamama

Princess, God's Wife, Queen, various - related to Osorkon II, Takelot II, Osorkon III.

Tentamenope, Ps
wife of Shoshenq III

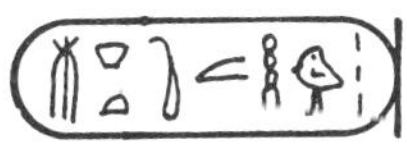

Meshentthemhu, Q
Mummy in royal cache of Deir el Bahri

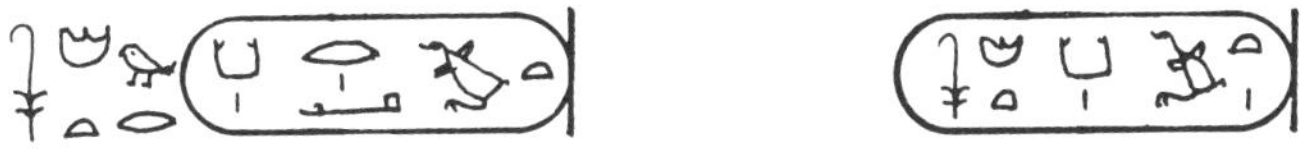

Karoatjet, Q - wife of Osorkon III

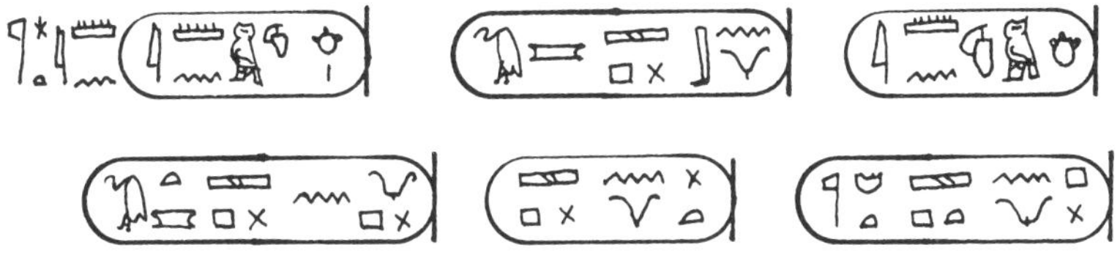

Khnumibamen - Shepenupet

Queen and God's Wife - daughter of Osorkon III

Tadibast, Q
wife of Shoshenq V

Tentkat . . . , Q
wife of Iuput I

4.10 REGISTER OF KINGS - LATE PERIOD

c 760-343 BC

25TH DYNASTY 760-657 BC (NUBIA-ETHIOPIAN)

760	Kashta	Maatre	126
747	Piankhy	Usermaatre Sneferre	126
716	Shabaka	Neferkare	126
702	Shebitku	Djedkaure	127
690	Taharqa	Nefertemkhure	127
664	Tantamani	Bakare	127

24TH/26TH DYNASTY 695-525 BC (SAIS)

695	Tefnakht II	Wahibre Iribre	128
688	Nekauba	Menibre	128
672	Necho I	Menkheperre	128
664	Psammetichus I	Wahibre	129
610	Necho II	Wehemibre	129
595	Psammetichus II	Neferibre	129
589	Apries	Haaibre/Wahibre	130
570	Amasis	Khnemibre	130
526	Psammetichus III	Ankhkaenre	130

27TH DYNASTY 525-405 BC (PERSIAN)

525	Cambyses	Mesutre	131
521	Darius I	Setutre	131
485	Xerxes I	Khshairsha	131
465	Khababash	Senenptahsetepentanen	132
464	Artabanos		132
464	Artaxerxes		132
424	Xerxes II		132
424	Darius II	Nebhebuserkhepeshmeryamen	133
405	Pedubast III	Seheribre	133

28TH DYNASTY 404-399 BC (SAIS)

404	Amyrataios		133

29TH DYNASTY 399-380 BC (MENDES)

399	Nepherites I	Baenre meryneferu	134
393	Psammuthis	Userre setepenptah	134
393	Hakoris	Khnemmaatre	134
380	Nepherites II		134

30TH DYNASTY 380-343 BC (SEBENNYTUS)

380	Nectanebo I	Kheperkare	135
362	Teos	Irmaatenre	135
360	Nectanebo II	Senedjemibre setepenamen	135

The Late Period began with more rivalry between the Nubian King Shabaka and the Sais king. Bochchoris of Sais being killed in an ensuing battle to end the 24th Dynasty.

The 25th Dynasty of Nubians then ruled all Egypt for a further 40 years. Under the rule of the Nubian King Taharqa, Necho from Sais was laying claim to the throne and through him the Assyrians eventually gained control for the 26th Dynasty, the last Nubian King Tantamani being driven out to end Nubia's brief kingship of Egypt. The Nubian kings retreated south to continue their kingship of Nubia from Napata and Meroe, still calling themselves Sons of Re and continuing their worship of the God Amen.

During the invasion by the Assyrians, local rulers of Egypt were again in force but Psammetichus, son of Necho, subdued them and the country united under one kingship again. Near the end of the 26th Dynasty Apries was usurped by his Vizier Amasis, but Persian eyes were on Egypt and, taking advantage of the unrest that followed, she invaded under Cambyses, defeating Amasis' successor Psammetichus III to place Egypt under Persian rule for the 27th Dynasty.

Egypt, in a state of disquiet, awaited its opportunity to return to native rule. This came via Amyrteos from Sais who rebelled, gained the Delta and eventually the rule of all Egypt. Unification was however, short lived, the 28th Dynasty consisted solely of his 5 year reign. Amyrteos' short rule was usurped by Nepherites I from Mendes, to found the 29th Dynasty. The blood line of this dynasty is not clear, but in any event they continued as sole rulers for only 19 years before the throne was once more usurped by another non-royal Nectanebo, a General from Sebennytus.

The 30th Dynasty was to be the last of the Pharaonic kingships. The only other Egyptian was Khababash, who ruled for a brief period, perhaps during the second Persian conquest. Thus the Egyptian Sons of Re expired, the Kingdom of Egypt had perished. The Ancient Chronicle's span of 36525 lunar years had been completed.

The 'Old Chronicle' was most likely a device concocted by the ancient priests, to try to emphasise Egypt's antiquity, and to explain its demise, hence its neatly convenient span of 36525 years (25 x 1461 lunar/solar cycles). The Chronicle was no doubt written after the event. See page 12.

KASHTA 25th Dynasty 760-747 BC

Maat Re Kashta

Not mentioned by Manetho. Brother of Alara, he was ruler of the Nubian Kingdom at Napata but probably had some influence as far north as Thebes. His son was Piankhy, future king of Egypt and founder of the 25th Dynasty. He was also the father of Shabaka, Piankhy's brother and successor to the Egyptian throne.

NUBIA

PIANKHY 25th Dynasty 747-716 BC

User Maat Re/Snefer Re Piankhy

Not mentioned by Manetho. King of Napata. Son of Kashta, he responded to the threat of Prince Tefnakht by invading Egypt. His victory stele names the Egyptian kings conquered and relates their capitulation. Piankhy did not stay in Egypt but returned to control Egypt from his native Nubia. He had a pyramid tomb at el Kurru.

Samtowe

NUBIA-ETHIOPIAN

SHABAKA 25th Dynasty 716-702 BC

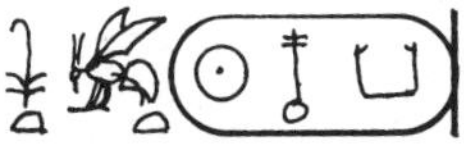

118
145

Nefer ka Re Sha ba ka

SABACON, M. When his brother Piankhy died, Shabaka came North, besieged Memphis, banished Bakenrenef (Bochchoris), said by Manetho to have burnt him alive, and stayed to rule all Egypt. This ended the Third Intermediate Period to begin the true Nubian domination of Egypt. He had a pyramid tomb at el Kurru.

Sebeqtowe

NUBIA-ETHIOPIAN

SHEBITKU 25th Dynasty 702-690 BC

Djed kau Re Sha ba ti ka

SEBICHOS, M. Son of Piankhy, he succeeded his uncle Shabaka. Nubia's rule of Egypt was firm, although some vassal kings ruled contemporaneously. His reign was peaceful but he supported Palestine against the Assyrians, nominating his brother Taharqa to lead his Egyptian-Nubian force. Buried in his pyramid tomb at El Kurru.

Djedkha NUBIA-ETHIOPIAN

TAHARQA 25th Dynasty 690-664 BC

Nefer tem khu Re Tah ar qa

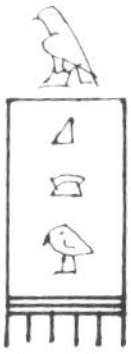

TARCUS, M. Son of Piankhy, brother of Shebitku, he ruled Egypt from Memphis. The Assyrian King Esarhaddon defeated Taharqa and claimed Egypt, but he died and Taharqa regained the kingship. Esarhaddon's successor Assurbanipal, then defeated Taharqa and he fled to Nubia. He had a pyramid tomb at Nuri.

Qakhau NUBIA-ETHIOPIAN

TANTAMANI 25th Dynasty 664-657 BC

Ba ka Re Tanta Amen

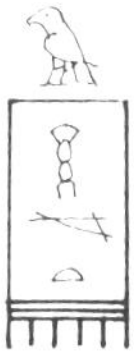

Son of Shebitku. In a dream he was told "Upper Egypt belongs to you, take to thyself Lower Egypt". He occupied Memphis after further battles with the Assyrians, but then lost Memphis, then Thebes and fled to Kipkipi. He ruled Upper Egypt but was contemporary with Psammetichus I in the North.

Wahmerit NUBIA-ETHIOPIAN

TEFNAKHT II 24th/26th Dynasty 695-688 BC

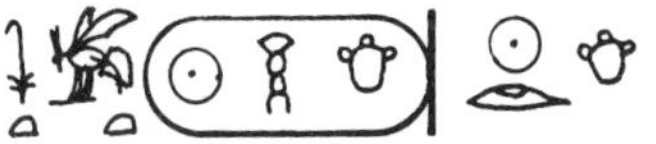
70
129

120

Wah ib Re/Ir ib Re Tef nakht

STEPHINATES, M. Equated by some with Manetho's Stephinates, Tefnakht II may have been a local king of Sais, possibly a descendant of Tefnakht I. His prenomen is equated doubtfully only from scarabs and beads. Otherwise nothing is known from the monuments. He may be the Menibre shown below.

SAIS

NEKAUBA 24th/26th Dynasty 688-672 BC

75

129

Men ib Re Ne kau ba

NECHEPSOS, M. The name Nekauba comes from an amulet and is equated by most with the above Manetho name. His lineage is unknown and no monuments of his have survived. His prenomen is unknown but has been identified by some with Menibre, a name found on scarabs of this period.

SAIS

NECHO I 26th Dynasty 672-664 BC

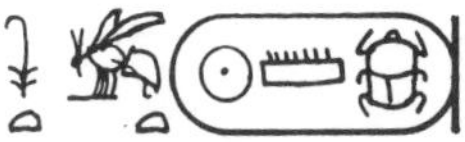
109
119

129

Men kheper Re Ne ka u

NECHAO, M. Probably a local king of Sais, his reign was probably ended by his death at the hands of Tantamani. He had probably been confirmed as ruler by Esarhaddon, the Assyrian king who had invaded Egypt earlier and was seeking to install local rulers as Assyrian vassals.

SAIS

PSAMMETICHUS I 26th Dynasty 664-610 BC

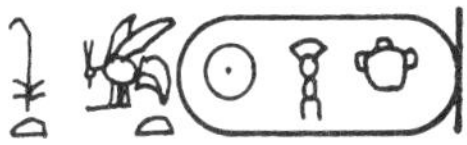
128
130

Wah ib Re

130

Ps em thek

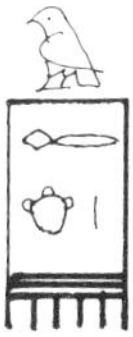
Aib

PSAMMETICHUS - reigned 54 years, M. Son of Necho I, he took the throne with the help of foreign mercenaries and set up garrisons to protect Egypt. His daughter Nitocris was adopted as God's Wife of Amen at Thebes. An oblisk in Rome has his name on it. His tomb is at Sais.

SAIS

NECHO II 26th Dynasty 610-595 BC

Weh em ib Re

128

Ne kau

Saib

NECHAO, M. Son of Psammetichus I. He maintained an army of Greeks and other foreigners. Planned a canal from the Nile at Bubastis, to the Red Sea (later completed by King Darius I). Fought battles against the Babylonians, first winning, but later losing all Syria and Palestine to them.

SAIS

PSAMMETICHUS II 26th Dynasty 595-589 BC

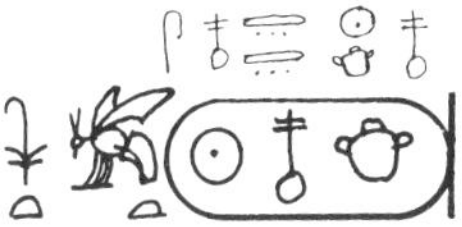
75
145

Nefer ib Re

130

Ps em thek

Menkhib

PSAMMUTHIS - reigned 6 years, M. Son of Necho II. His daughter Ankhnesneferibre was adopted as God's Wife, Priestess of Amen at Thebes. He invaded and defeated the Nubians. His cartouches are found in many places throughout Egypt. Sarcophagus found at Damanhur.

SAIS

APRIES 26th Dynasty 589-570 BC

128
129

Ha a ib Re — Wah ib Re

Wahib

UAPHRIS - son of Psammuthis, he reigned 19 years, M. King Hophra of the Bible. Following heavy losses in a battle against the Babylonians, he sent his General Amasis to quell a rebellion of Egyptians. Amasis later usurped the throne to become the next king. Tomb in the el Asasif at Thebes.

SAIS

AMASIS 26th Dynasty 570-526 BC

90

Khnem ib Re — Ah mose

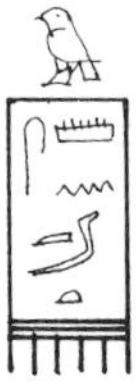

Smenmaat

AMOSIS - reigned 44 years, M. A non-royal, he usurped the throne after being Apries' General. He was the official husband of Ankhnesneferibre, daughter of Psammetichus II. Thus he tried to legitimise the throne. He caused ill-feeling with the Persians, probably bringing about the Persian invasion of Egypt.

SAIS

PSAMMETICHUS III 26th Dynasty 526-525 BC

144

129

Ankh ka en Re — Ps em thek

Wepahtowe

PSAMMECHERITES - son of Amosis, reigned 6 months, M. Lost the battle of Bedusian, after which Egypt passed into the hands of the Persians. He can be seen in a relief at Karnak, standing in the presence of the Gods Amen, and Horus son of Isis and Osiris.

SAIS

CAMBYSES 27th Dynasty 525-522 BC

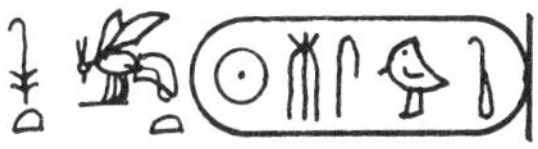

Mes ut Re

Cam by ses

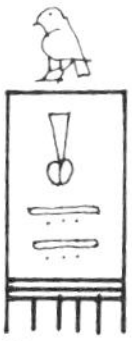

CAMBYSES, M. A Persian, the son of Cyrus conqueror of Babylon. He invaded and settled his people in Egypt. A wicked man, he mutilated the tombs and temples, and committed many atrocities. He returned to Persia and left a Governor Aryandes in charge. Cambyses is supposed to have committed suicide.

Samtowe

PERSIAN

DARIUS I 27th Dynasty 521-486 BC

Set ut Re

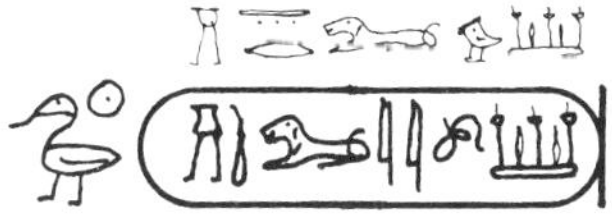

133

Antry usha (Darius)

DARIUS son of Hystapes - reigned 37 years, M. King of Persia after Cambyses and a usurper Smerdis. He returned to Egypt and put to death Aryandes, who he thought had rebelled. He set up a school for scribes and restored the temples, priests and gods. Finished the canal between the Nile and the Red Sea.

PERSIAN

XERXES I 27th Dynasty 485-465 BC

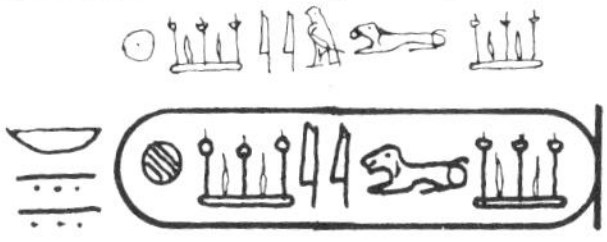

Kh shair sha

Xer xes

XERXES - son of Darius, he reigned 21 years, M. During his reign the Egyptians rebelled under King Khababash. Xerxes visited Egypt to end the revolt and restore the Persian rule. He left his brother Achemenes in charge and returned to Persia. He was murdered by his bodyguard at Susa, Captain of the guard, Artabanos.

PERSIAN

KHABABASH 27th Dynasty c 465 BC

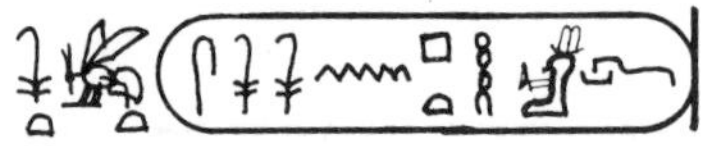 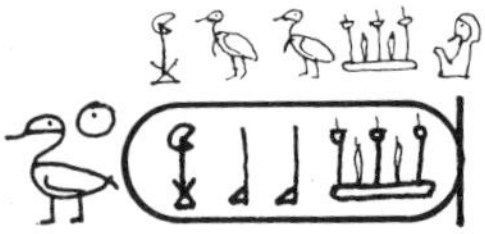

Senen Ptah setepen Tanen Kha baba sh

Not mentioned by Manetho. Reigned for little over a year. He was the leader of Egyptian revolt during the reign of Xerxes I. He tried to take advantage of the war between Persia and Greece. Began to fortify Egypt's frontiers. Position not certain, he may have been the last Egyptian Pharaoh, rather than Nectanebo II.

PERSIAN

ARTABANOS 27th Dynasty c 464 BC

ARTABANUS - reigned 7 months, M. He was the murderer of Xerxes I at Susa in Persia. Not known of in Egypt, but shown in Manetho's Kings List. No cartouche names have been found.

PERSIAN

ARTAXERXES 27th Dynasty 464-424 BC

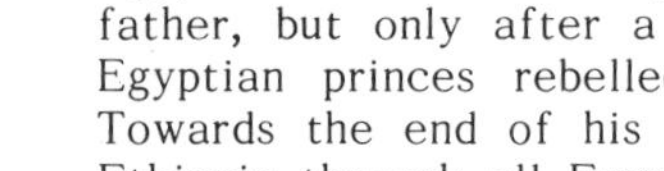 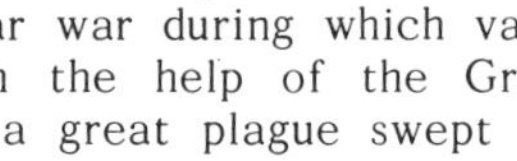

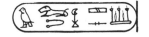

Ar ta kha sha sha Ar ta kha sha sha

ARTAXERXES - son of Xerxes, M. Took the throne of Egypt after a troubled period, following the death of his father, but only after a 6 year war during which various Egyptian princes rebelled with the help of the Greeks. Towards the end of his reign a great plague swept from Ethiopia through all Egypt.

PERSIAN

XERXES II 27th Dynasty c 424 BC

XERXES - son of Artaxerxes. Reigned 2 months, M. After succeeding his father he was murdered by his half-brother Sogdianus, but Sogdianus only reigned 7 months and was also murdered by his brother Ochus (Darius II). Of Xerxes II nothing else is known and no cartouches have been found.

PERSIAN

DARIUS II 27th Dynasty 424-405 BC

131

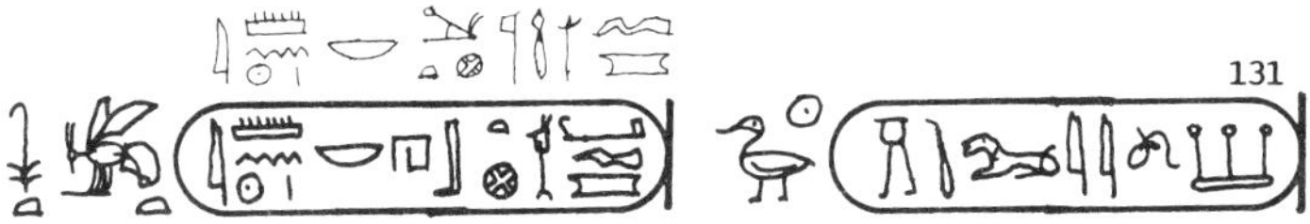

Neb heb user khepesh mery Amen Antry usha (Darius)

DARIUS - son of Xerxes II, M. This reign saw the end of the first Persian dominance. Little is known about him, except that he was called Nothus because he may have been one of 17 illegitimate sons of King Artaxerxes. He married Darysis, daughter of Xerxes I. Murdered his brother Sogdianus. Last Persian with a cartouche.

PERSIAN

PEDUBAST III c 405 BC

116
121

Seher ib Re Pedu Bast

This king probably reigned during this period, but very little evidence of him has been found. His name appears on some scarabs.

AMYRATAIOS 28th Dynasty 404-399 BC

AMYRTEOS - reigned 6 years, M. He came from a family of the hereditary princes of the Delta. Helped the Egyptians to regain their independance during the reign of Darius II. He had a son Pausaris, but he did not come to the throne.

SAIS

NEPHERITES I 29th Dynasty 399-393 BC

Ba en Re mery neteru Nai f au rud

NEPHERITES - reigned 6 years, M. Little is known of this king but a few items bear his cartouche and a stele from Karnak is inscribed with his name.

MENDES

PSAMMUTHIS 29th Dynasty c 393 BC

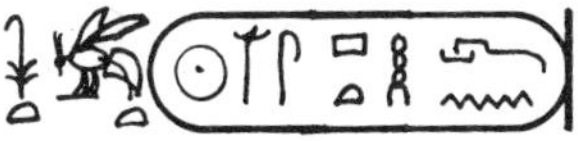

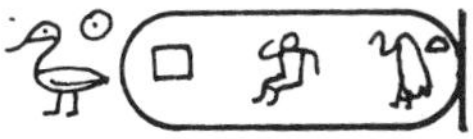

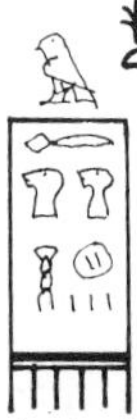

User Re setepen Ptah Ps a Mut

PSAMMUTHIS - reigned one year, M. Little is known of him, his reign was contemporary with the first year of Achoris. He is seen on a slab (Berlin Museum), making offerings to the Gods Amen and Khonsu.

Apiethiwassapu

MENDES

HAKORIS 29th Dynasty 393-380 BC

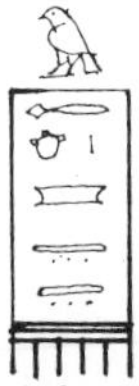

Khnem Maat Re Ha koris

ACHORIS - reigned 13 years, M. He repaired many of the temples at Thebes and his name is found at Karnak, and in the quarries of Tura. He helped the king of Cyprus with provisions in a battle against the Persians, and thus probably laid the foundations for the next Persian invasion.

Aibmerytowe

MENDES

NEPHERITES II 29th Dynasty c 380 BC

Son of Achoris. According to Manetho King Nepherites reigned for only 4 months.

NECTANEBO I 30th Dynasty 380-362 BC

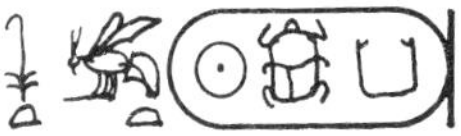
58
145

Kheper ka Re Nekht neb ef

NECTANEBES - reigned 18 years, M. He built many monuments and additions to existing temples. Waged war against the Persians and held off another occupation of Egypt by them. He was succeeded by his son, who was named Teos after his grandfather.

Demaat SEBENNYTUS

TEOS 30th Dynasty 362-360 BC

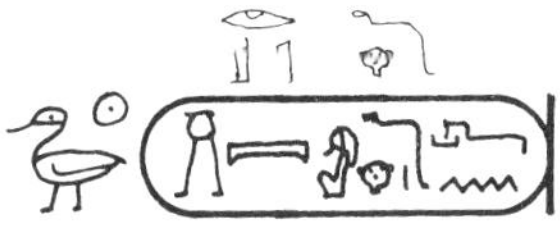

Ir Maat en Re Teos

TACHOS. **TEOS** - reigned 2 years, M. He built up a large army and waged war against Phoenicia. Others supported Nekhtharehbe and Teos was usurped, fleeing to Persia where he eventually died in exile. Nekhtharehbe thus became the next and last Pharaoh of Egypt.

Khaemmaatsamtowe SEBENNYTUS

NECTANEBO II 30th Dynasty 360-343 BC

Se nedjem ib Re setepen Amen Nekht har eh be

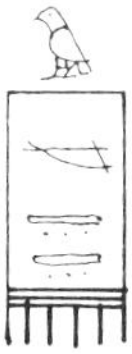

NECTANBUS - reigned 18 years, M. Said to have been the son of Nectanebo I. He carried out much building and maintained a large army. Probably the last true Egyptian Pharaoh (but see Khababash, page 132). Under him however, Egypt fell once again to the Persians. The Great Empire was finished.

Merytowe SEBENNYTUS

QUEENS, PRINCESSES AND GOD'S WIVES OF THIS PERIOD

Pebatmar, Q - sister/wife of Kashta

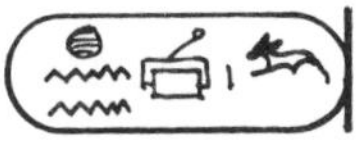

Khensa, Q - daughter of Kashta, wife of Piankhy

Amenirdis, Q - daughter of Kashta. (Another as daughter of Taharqa)

Abar, Q
sister/wife of Piankhy

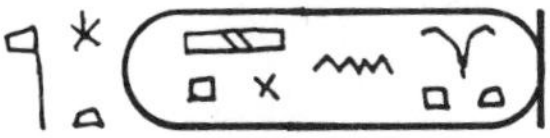

Shepenupet - Hentneferumut - Iretre
God's Wife of Amen - daughter of Piankhy

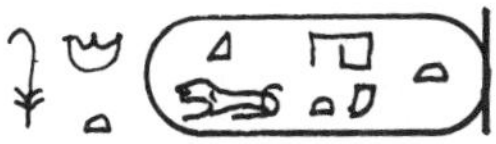

Qalhata, Q
sister/wife of Shebitku

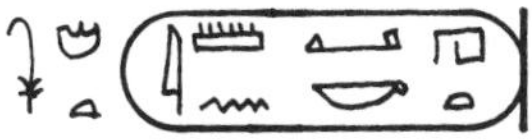

Tekahatamani, Q
sister/wife of Taharqa

Aqlaq, Q
mother of Taharqa

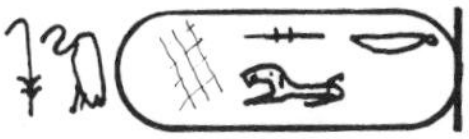

. . . Salka Q
wife of Taharqa

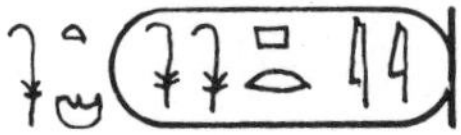

Naparaye, Q
sister/wife of Taharqa

Atakhebasken, Q
wife of Taharqa

QUEENS, PRINCESSES AND GOD'S WIVES OF THIS PERIOD

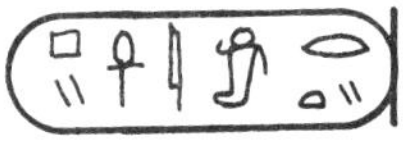

Picankharty, Q
sister/wife of Tantamani

Akhresan, Q

Mehtenweskhet, Q
wife of Psammetichus I

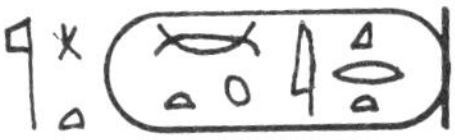

48

Netaqert, Ps (Nitocris)
daughter of Psammetichus I

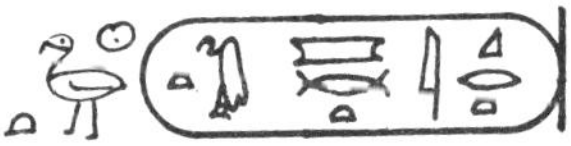

Netaqertmerymut - Nebneferumut
God's Wife of Amen - daughter of Psammetichus I

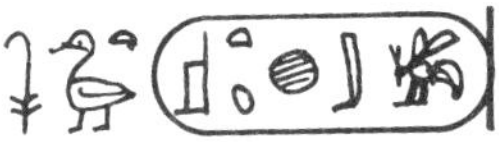

Istemkheb, Ps
daughter of Psammetichus II

Takhauth, Q
wife of Psammetichus II

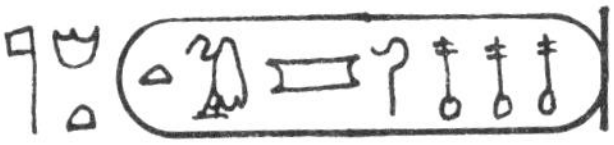

Ankhnesneferibre - Heqaneferumerymut
God's Wife of Amen - daughter of Psammetichus II
(Another Ankhnesneferibre as daughter of Psammetichus I)

Tefnutmery, Q

Tasheretist, Ps
mother of Ahmose

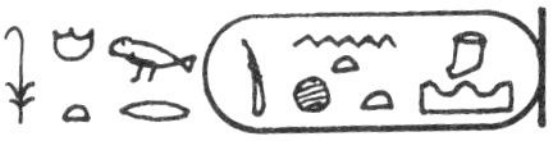

Thentkheta, Q
wife of Ahmose

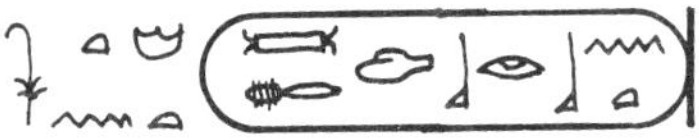

Netkhetedaribent, Q
wife of Nectanebo

5.01 EGYPTIAN QUEENS, PRINCES AND PRINCESSES

The kings' wives, sons, and daughters also had their names in cartouches. Thus there are numerous cartouches of non-kings. These can usually be recognised as such by the prefix indicating the status of the person named in the cartouche.

Eg. King's wife 

King's son 

King's daughter 

God's Wife 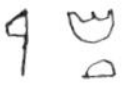

A list of these prefixes is given on page 157.

I have included a comprehensive selection of the 'non king' cartouches, and these are disposed at the end of each dynastic period as follows:-

It should be noted that the above selection is based on the cartouches of better known personages. Of the others, they will usually be found in association with the relevant king, so the reader may be able to at least determine a family connection.

5.02 LATE PERSIAN PERIOD AND GRECO-ROMAN RULERS

2nd Persian Period 343-332 BC
343 Artaxerxes III Ochus
338 Arses
335 Darius III Codoman

GRECO-ROMAN PERIOD
332 BC - 395 AD

Macedonian Dynasty
332 Alexander the Great
323 Philip Arrhidaeus
316 Alexander IV

Ptolemaic Dynasty
304 Ptolemy I Soter I
285 Ptolemy II Philadelphus
246 Ptolemy III Euergetes I
221 Ptolemy IV Philopator
205 Ptolemy V Epiphanes
180 Ptolemy VI Philometor
170 Ptolemy VIII Euergetes II (Physkon)
145 Ptolemy VII Neos Philopator
116 Cleopatra III Q and Ptolemy IX Soter II (Lathyros)
107 Cleopatra III Q and Ptolemy X Alexander I
88 Ptolemy IX Soter II
81 Cleopatra Berenice Q
80 Ptolemy XI Alexander II
80 Ptolemy XII Neos Dionysos (Auletes)
58 Berenice IV Q
51 Cleopatra VII Q
51 Ptolemy XIII
47 Ptolemy XIV
44 Ptolemy XV Caesarion

Roman Emperors 30 BC-395 AD
30 Augustus
14 Tiberius
37 Gaius (Caligula)
41 Claudius
54 Nero
68 Galba
69 Otho
69 Vespasian
79 Titus
81 Domitian
96 Nerva
98 Trajan
117 Hadrian
138 Antonius Pius
161 Marcus Aurelius
161 Lucius Verus
180 Commodus
193 Septimius Severus
198 Caracalla
209 Geta
217 Macrinus
218 Diadumenianus
222 Severus Alexander
238 Gordian III
244 Philip
249 Decius
251 Gallus and Volusianus
253 Valerian
253 Gallienus
260 Macrianus and Quietus
270 Aurelian
276 Probus
284 Diocletian
286 Maximian
293 Galerius

The above list is based on the one that appears in the ATLAS OF ANCIENT EGYPT (Baines & Malek), published in the UK by Phaidon Press Ltd.

5.02 LATE PERSIAN PERIOD AND GRECO-ROMAN RULERS

LATE PERSIAN PERIOD

After King Nectanebo II had fled in terror to Ethiopia from the invading King Ochus, Egypt fell once more to the Persians, never again to be ruled by an Egyptian Pharaoh.

The usurper Khababash, a native Egyptian king, may have reigned during this period or during the 27th Dynasty (see page 132), but his position is not known for certain.

Manetho did not list these kings of the Second Persian Period, but they were added to his list by later chronologists and called the 31st Dynasty.

GRECO-ROMAN RULERS

A few native rulers claimed the throne during the Greco-Roman Period, but these were only in effect Governors, not kings.

Alexander the Great reached Egypt in 332 BC to effect his rule. The following foreign rulers of Egypt also used the title 'Son of Re', and they continued the traditions of the Egyptians and worshipped their gods. They built many temples and their cartouches are to be found throughout Egypt.

Most of their cartouches are quite distinct from those of the Pharaohs, and the reader can distinguish the cartouches of these foreign rulers from those of the Pharaonic Egyptians by following the simple guidelines given below:-

The Ptolemaic kings' cartouches contain the following group of signs, not found as a group in Pharaonic cartouches.

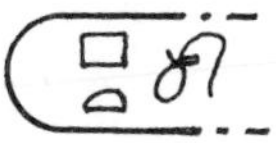 VARIANT  OR 

Eg. **PTOLEMY** 

So that any cartouche with this group in it, belongs to a PTOLEMY.

The cartouches of the three Macedonian kings are shown below:-

ALEXANDER THE GREAT

PHILIP ARRHIDAEUS

ALEXANDER IV

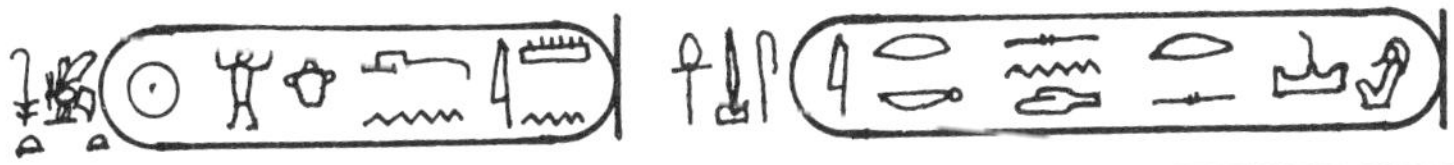

The cartouches of the Ptolemaic Queens and Princesses are shown below:-

BERENICE I

wife of Ptolemy I

ARSINOE I

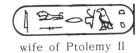

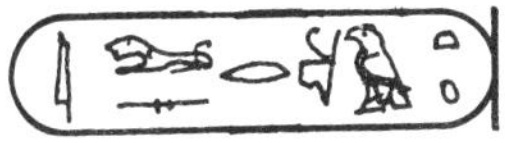

wife of Ptolemy II

ARSINOE II

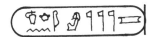

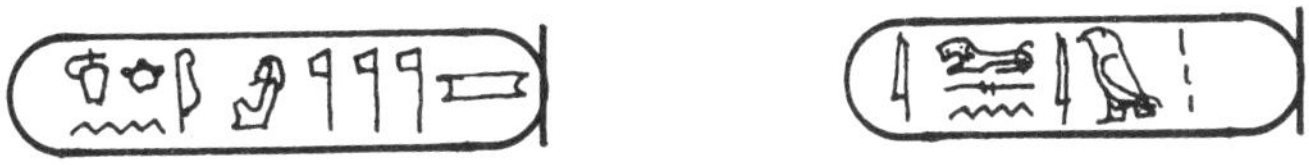

PHILOTERA

daughter of Ptolemy I

BERENICE II

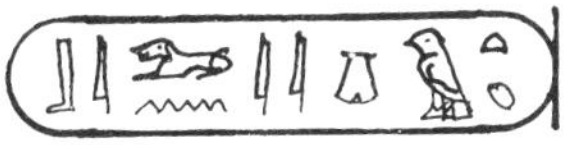

wife of Ptolemy III

BERENICE III

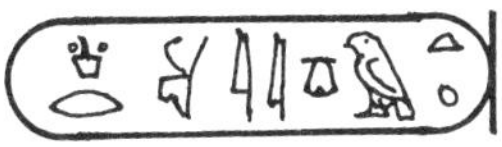

daughter of Ptolemy III

ARSINOE III

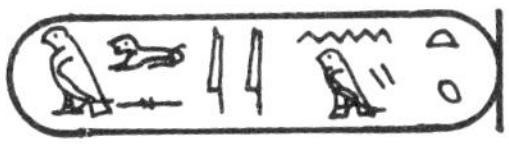

wife of Ptolemy IV

CLEOPATRA I

wife of Ptolemy V

CLEOPATRA II

wife of Ptolemy VII

CLEOPATRA III - wife of Ptolemy IX

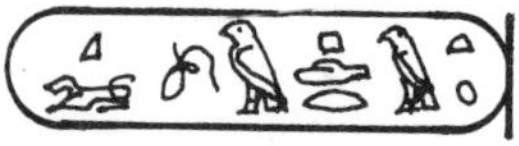

CLEOPATRA IV - BERENICE IV - wife of Ptolemy XI

CLEOPATRA VI

wife of Ptolemy XIII

CLEOPATRA VII

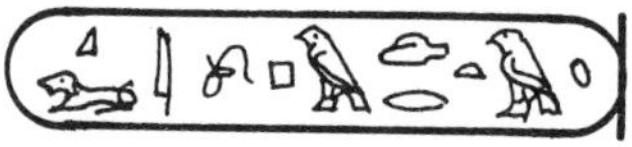

ROMAN EMPERORS

The cartouches of the Roman Emperors contained the title **Autkrtr** and/or **Kaisrs.** These titles are identified by their group signs as follows:-

Autkrtr

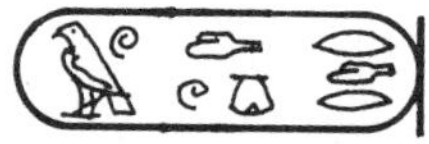

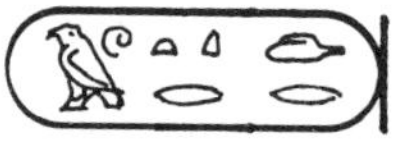

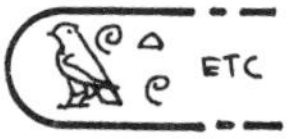

Thus you need only look for the group signs

Kaisrs

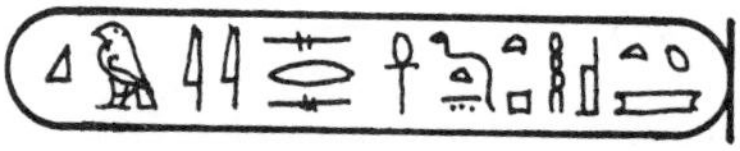

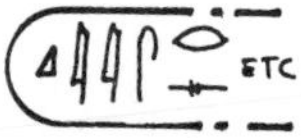

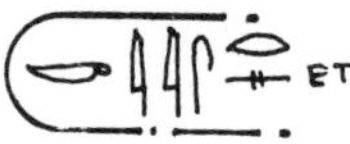

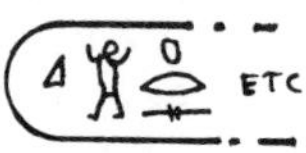

Thus, if the cartouche contains any of the above groups it belongs to a Roman Emperor rather than an Egyptian Pharaoh.

5.03 CONTEMPORARY KINGS OF NUBIA

Throughout history Egypt has considered Nubia, or Kush as they came to call it, as the country that supplied gold and slaves. They coveted it for this reason and sought to possess it as part of their kingdom. As Egypt's fortunes fluctuated, so did their possession of Kush. Battles between the two countries invariably resulted in a conquest by Egypt, and the early Kushite culture was thus very much influenced by Egypt.

The Palermo Stone records that King Seneferu of the 4th Dynasty sent his army into 'the Land of the Blacks'. Many other kings exerted their power in Nubia and erected monuments recording their sovereignty there.

After the rise of the God Amen-Re in the 12th Dynasty, many later kings dedicated temples to this god in Nubia, in fact Thebes, the domain of the High Priest of Amen, seemed to have had a special relationship with the Nubian. With the curtailment of the priests' activities in the 22nd Dynasty, some fled to Nubia and were welcomed there as the leaders of the Amen cult.

The decline of Egypt's overall power after the New Kingdom, possibly reflected itself in Nubia, which began to establish its own sovereignty under Kashta, King of Napata, brother of Alara. It was probably under the influence of the exiled priests of Amen that he cast envious eyes on Thebes, and considered it as part of his sovereignty, but it was under the next Nubian King Piankhy, son of Kashta, that the Nubians, or Ethiopians as Manetho called them, conquered and ruled over all Egypt.

The Nubian rule of Egypt ended with the flight back of Tantamani after his defeat at Memphis. Egypt, however, no longer claimed Nubia and the Nubian kingship continued from Napata then later Meroe, contemporaneously with the Egyptian and Greco-Roman kings until 339 AD.

In the period immediately following the ancestral King Alara and the 25th Dynasty, the Nubian rulers adopted the Egyptian tradition of having two cartouche names. Although the names are often difficult to equate to Egyptian hieroglyphs, they sometimes copied earlier Egyptian names. I have therefore included these, together with the complementary prenomen, to enable the reader to distinguish them from the Pharaonic kings.

As the separate Nubian Kingdom developed, the use of old Egyptian names diminished, and both the prenomen and nomen became completely Nubianised, and in fact even today very little is known of the Meroitic language. Very few of the Nubian cartouches are found in Egypt.

CONTEMPORARY KINGS OF NUBIA

KING - ATLANERSA - son of Taharqa

Khu ka Re

Atlanersa

KING - SENKAMANISKEN - son of Atlanersa

Se kheper Re

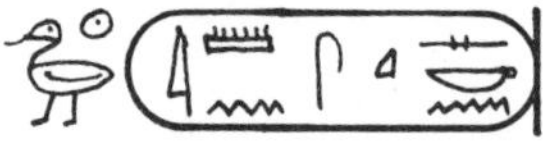
Senkamanisken

KING - ANLAMANI - son of Senkamanisken

146

Ankh ka Re

Anlamani

KING - ASPELTA - son of Senkamanisken

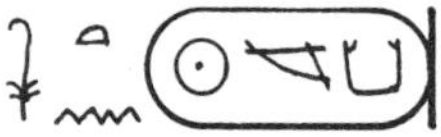
53

Mery ka Re

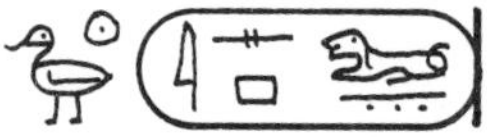
Aspelta

KING - AMTALQA - son of Aspelta

80
86

Wadj ka Re

Amtalqa

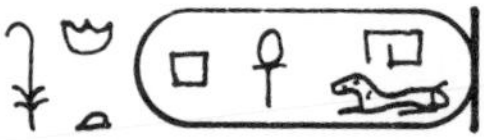
Pi ankh hor - Queen

KING - MALENAQEN - son of Amtalqa

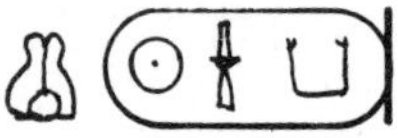
64
86

Sekhem ka Re

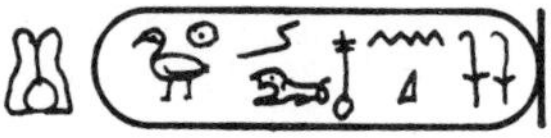
Malenaqen

CONTEMPORARY KINGS OF NUBIA

KING - ANALMAATYE

126

Nefer ka Re

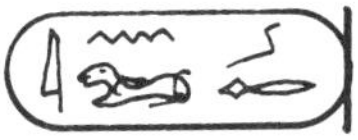

Analmaatye

KING - AMANI-NATAKI-LEBTE

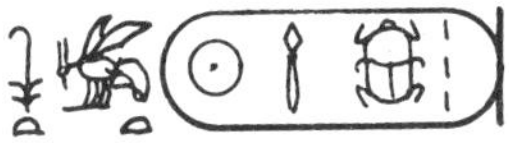

92

A kheperu Re

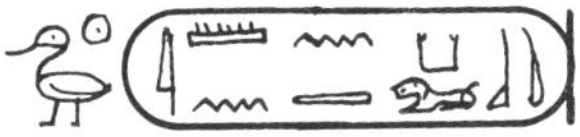

Amani-Nataki-Lebte

KING - PIANKHARITEN - c Amani-Nataki-Lebte

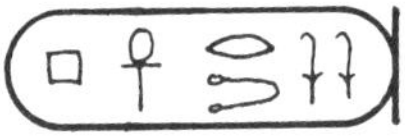

Pi ankh arit en

KING - AMANIASTABARQA

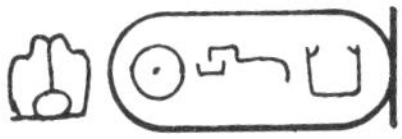

Setep ka Re

Amaniastabarqa

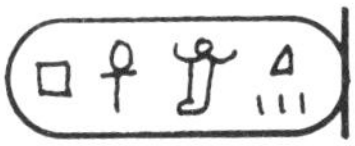

Pi ankh qew qa - Queen

KING - MALEWIEBAMANI - son of Nasakhma

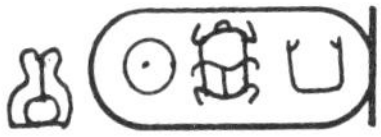

135
146

Kheper ka Re

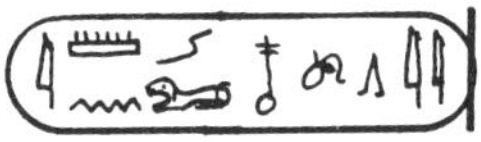

Malewiebamani

KING AMAN-NETE-YERIKE - son of Malewiebamani

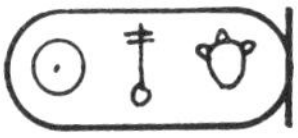

75
129

Nefer ib Re

Aman-Nete-Yerike

CONTEMPORARY KINGS OF NUBIA

P el kha - Queen

KING - NASTASEN - son of Pelkha

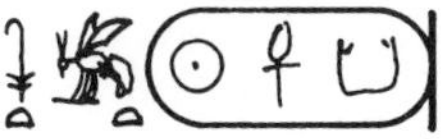

144

Ankh ka Re

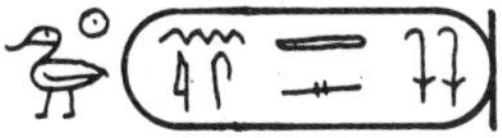

Nastasen

KING - NATAKAMANI

135
145

Kheper ka Re

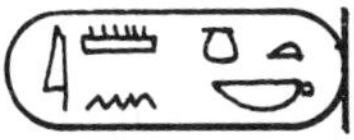

Natakamani

PRINCE - ARIKANKHARER - son of Natakamani

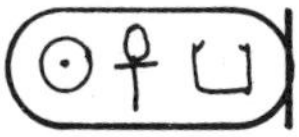

144

Ankh ka Re

Arikankharer

KING - ERGAMENES (MURTEK)

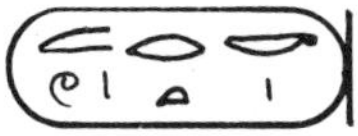

Murtek

Ergamenes

KING - TEQERIDEAMANI - son of Aretanide

135
145

Kheper ka Re

Teqerideamani

KING - TAHANAMAMANI

92

Neb Maat Re

Tahanamamani

5.04 MISCELLANEOUS

UNKNOWN KINGS

Cartouches are often found on small relics such as scarabs, rings, cylinder seals, statuettes, amulets, etc. In some cases these cartouches have not been identified with known kings. They may therefore belong to unknown kings or may be variants of known kings. Occasionally they may belong to non-royal persons. Sometimes the relic bears the cartouche only, without a prefix to determine its status. A selection of cartouches from such relics is given below:-

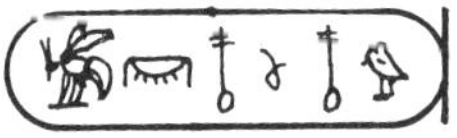

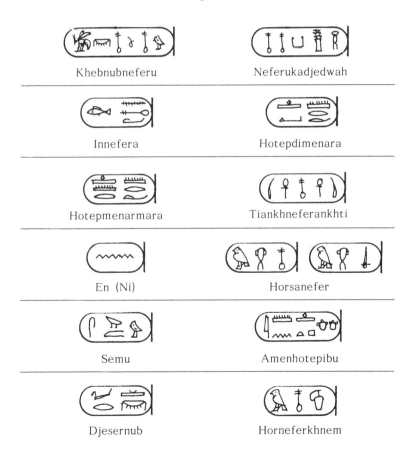

Khebnubneferu

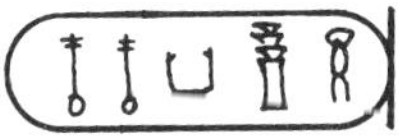

Neferukadjedwah

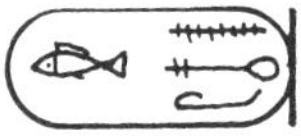

Innefera

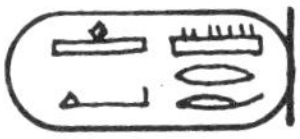

Hotepdimenara

Hotepmenarmara

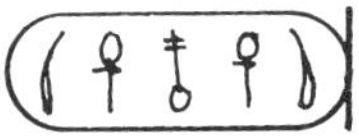

Tiankhneferankhti

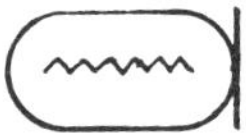

En (Ni)

Horsanefer

Semu

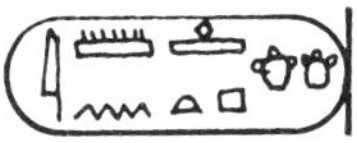

Amenhotepibu

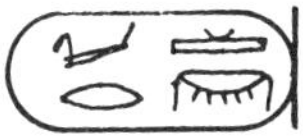

Djesernub

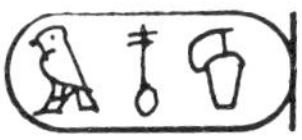

Horneferkhnem

Smakare

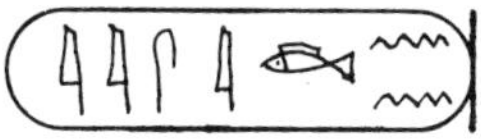

Yisnet

Minor Hyksos kings

Herwemeyes

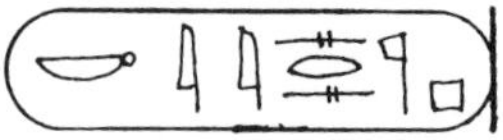

Keyseresnetep

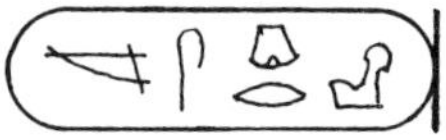

Merseker, Q

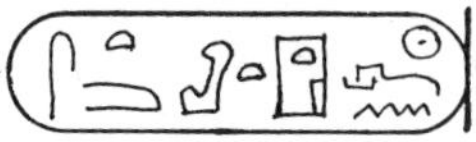

Setemhathorsetepenre
(c Herihor)

OTHERS

Cartouches were sometimes used for dedications to gods and other miscellaneous uses, but these were usually associated with the specific king or god, eg.,

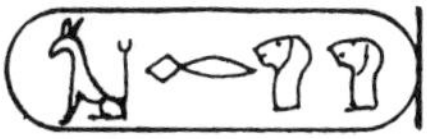

Setapeh

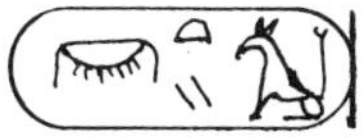

Nubti

The God Set of Ombos

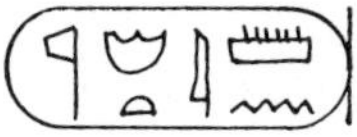

God's Wife of Amen

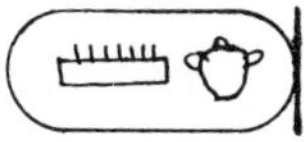

Menib
(Pyramid of Menkauhor)

6 CARTOUCHE IDENTIFICATION SYSTEM

The system is based on comparing signs in the cartouche being read, with those on the grid charts.

Identification of a cartouche can be made in three simple steps:-

1. Determine which grid chart to use.
2. Locate the cartouche page number on the chart.
3. Compare the cartouche with those on the page.

1. The correct grid chart is determined by spotting the signs as follows:-

A. Use **CHART A** if the cartouche contains any of the following group signs. 

B. Use **CHART B** if the cartouche contains any figure of a god or man (standing or seated). For example,

Viz, any figures of Gods/Men.

C. Use **CHART C** if the cartouche contains a circle ○ plus three or less signs in total and does not fit **CHART A or B.**

Any circle, eg., ○ or ⊙ or ⊘

D. Use **CHART D** if the cartouche contains a circle ○ plus four or more signs in total and does not fit **CHART A** or **B.**

Any circle, eg., ○ or ⊙ or ⊘

E. Use **CHART E** if the cartouche does not contain a circle ⊙ and does not fit **CHART A** or **B.**

CHARTS C, D and **E** should <u>**ONLY**</u> be used when the cartouche does not fit **CHART A** or **B.**

2. The correct page number is found by reading the cartouche starting at the opposite end from the bar. The first sign from the cartouche which is on the respective chart is used as the first co-ordinate, the second co-ordinate is either the relevant group sign or the relevant God/Man (Chart A or B), or the next sign in the cartouche. The intersection of the two co-ordinates gives the cartouche page number.

Most cartouches can be located by means of the first three signs, but some may need to use the other signs. The method is the same however, for all cartouches - locate the first sign in the cartouche on the chart and try the next signs in order until an intersection is found.

3. Turn to the cartouche page and compare the cartouche with those on the page. If an exact match is found, then you have identified the cartouche. If an exact match is not found, return to the location chart and check out the next page number at the same intersection point. The intersection point contains a few numbers, but the first number reached from the first sign in the cartouche is usually the correct one. See examples on opposite page.

NOTE - The reference numbers at the side of the cartouches refer to other pages with the same cartouche names. In this case the complimentary NOMEN or PRENOMEN cartouche must be sought to make a positive identification of the king.

For each major king I have included some popular versions of his name as well as the classical Greek name (in bold) derived from the High Priest Manetho. The letter **M** denotes this name or any extract from Manetho's 'History of Egypt'. Under each cartouche the name has been broken into syllables to aid pronunciation. The Egyptian language did not use vowels, so it is left to the translator to include them where necessary. My versions are compromise to cater for the wide variety that have been used by different authorities.

Only the main elements of the king's personal name are given, since the additional signs, sometimes combined with it, represent epithets which often vary from cartouche to cartouche.

I have not included direct transliteration, since it would be meaningless to the general reader - the student and qualified Egyptologist will be able to read the hieroglyphs anyway.

The name of the discoverer or excavator of the tomb is given in brackets. The king's place of origin or his capital city, is given at the bottom right-hand corner. The king's Horus name is given at the bottom left-hand corner.

EXAMPLES OF CARTOUCHE LOCATION

EXAMPLE 1

Group signs

CHART A

First sign in cartouche is also the group sign 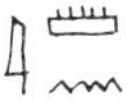

Next sign in cartouche which is also on Chart A is 
Intersection point gives Page 109/110. 110 = PSUSENNES I.

EXAMPLE 2a

Gods/Men in cartouche and also on Chart

CHART B

First sign in cartouche which is also on Chart B is 

Next sign in cartouche is the relevant God/Man sign 
Intersection point gives Page 95 = AY.

EXAMPLE 2b

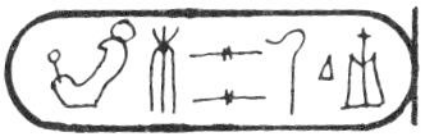

Gods/Men in cartouche but not on Chart

CHART B

First sign in cartouche which is also on Chart B is 

Next sign in cartouche which is also on Chart B is 
Intersection point gives Page 98 = RAMESSES III.

EXAMPLE 3

⊙ + 3 or less signs

CHART C

First sign in cartouche which is also on Chart C is 

Next sign in cartouche which is also on Chart C is ☥
Intersection point gives Page 57 = MENTUHOTEP II.

EXAMPLE 4

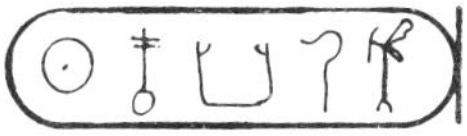

⊙ + 4 or more signs

CHART D

First sign in cartouche which is also on Chart D is 

Next sign in cartouche which is also on Chart D is 
Intersection point gives Page 110 = AMENEMNISU.

EXAMPLE 5

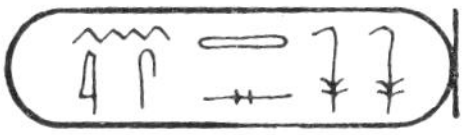

Not fitting other charts

CHART E

First sign in cartouche which is also on Chart E is 

Next sign in cartouche which is also on Chart E is 
Intersection point gives Page 146 = NASTASEN.

CHART A - CARTOUCHES CONTAINING ANY OF THE FOLLOWING GROUP SIGNS.

	18 91 123	114 90,147	117,114 97,99,98					
	90 147	116 71		96				
	100/1 136 104,106,99	96 147		97		97		
	109 122 123 111			22				
	121	112, 99 114	115	105,101 96, 57	83	121 101		
	67 110 145	68, 69	110	96 42, 45	68, 65	145		
	18 109 146 133	87, 57				135 94		
	58 67 114	80				111 110		
	18 117 145 136	102, 87 81 70			93	112		
	95 109 141 110		115 116			141		
	99, 98,97 116 113	116,111 81	116, 97 100	71		117,111,96 116,114,98 106,134,99		
	105 106 144	68,121 58 65		82 76 75		118 113 132 135		
	98 102 103 111	69		97 102	93,103	97 95 100		
	94 104	113 98 118,116	114		93 94 104	141		
	127,112,99 118 145	112,114 116 96	127		112 68	113 141 99		
	105, 61,65 126,144,66 145 146	147 58 48 55	102 73	76,118 97 18 29		118 101		
	111	96	61,134	97 96 91,109	82	101 109 111 112		
	122	112 66		73				
				29	75			

CHART B - CARTOUCHES CONTAINING FIGURES OF GODS/MEN AND NOT FITTING CHART A.

18 19 106
20 95 98 96,122 106 99 92 98 96 100 99 122 96 96 91 96 76 134 106
68,102 122 105 98 20 19 104 146 21
21 66 20 75,76,136 65,70, 72
38 38 105 100 19 103 97 60 121
67 84 100 44,42 120 106 73 137 103 97,98/9 100,106
109 21 104 18 21
17 21,137 145,100 137 99
121 51 76 21 22 67 21 122 49 91 146
34 18 79 103 93,135 104 132 103 104
122, 21 95 104 20 19 104 104 21
122 19 95 141 19
76 22 17 52 101 99 101
99 106 57 100 106 111 110,111 103 100 20
104 19 134 103 111 106 105 103
21 76 21 103 91
31

CHART C - CARTOUCHES CONTAINING ◯+ 3 OR LESS SIGNS AND NOT FITTING CHART A OR B.

34									
	58 135 127	52 91 45 80	86 75 80	72 131 43	144 71 86	38,47,127 83,34,118	59,69,130 42 144	41	
	93 72	34 83 118 52	75,129	71 51 79	71	106	44 69	44	
	59 109	59 69		58		44 69 41	66	69 75 42 59	
	144	72	133 66 82	99 87		51 71 79	57 65 58 82		
	93 71	130,144 134	130	57 82 65	71		82 66		
		58	91 92 90 85	144 94		93	93 59		
	81	59 79	80 79	80		80	42 75 69 59		
	85 112	86 64 80		66,64,84 82 75	70	73 64	86 69		
	91,92,119 128 95	42 90 144	75,128			64	95		
	94 79	38,148 92		74	78	57 104	90	83	
	119	67	129		73 47 71	43 52			
		53,120	70 86 129	72 85					
	41 75	45,127 113	78	77 46 80 126	77	72	71	41	
			60	86 126				77	
	58	51 80			47				
		127 96	86						
		61 68	6.6 80	86		61	69		

CHART D - CARTOUCHES CONTAINING ○ + 4 OR MORE SIGNS AND NOT FITTING CHART A OR B.

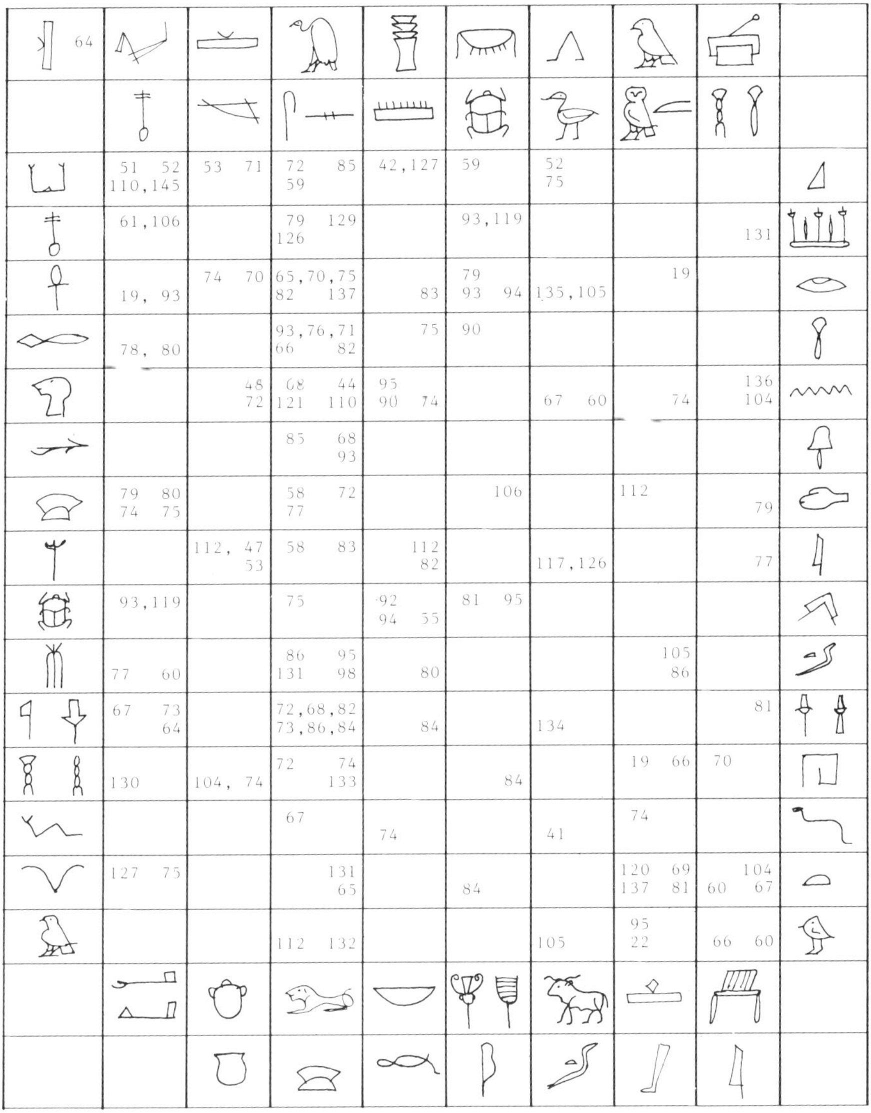

64
51 52 110,145
53 71
72 85 59
42,127
59
52 75
61,106
79 129 126
93,119
131
19, 93
74 70
65,70,75 82 137
83
79 93 94
135,105
19
78, 80
93,76,71 66 82
75
90
48 72
68 44 121 110
95 90 74
67 60
74
136 104
85 68 93
79 80 74 75
58 72 77
106
112
79
112, 47 53
58 83
112 82
117,126
77
93,119
75
92 94 55
81 95
77 60
86 95 131 98
80
105 86
67 73 64
72,68,82 73,86,84
84
134
81
130
104, 74
72 74 133
84
19 66
70
67
74
41
74
127 75
131 65
84
120 69 137 81
104 60 67
112 132
105
95 22
66 60

CHART E - CARTOUCHES NOT CONTAINING ○ AND NOT FITTING CHART A OR B.

19	147					60 20			30
	68 115 121		77 60		131			54	
	123 137 147	29,37,106 52 131	147 36	32	105 44 35	144			
		105 102 122	146		81	20,119,47 122 103	105 43	22 66	
60 20	31,134,141 51,132,147	87,98,120 137,114,21	76 147	19 76 134	45 71 20 81	76 119 20,47, 45	18 38	20	
	46 19	68 87	113	148	34			80 118 46	
	128 127 126 21	21	30 33 52 148		21	51 122 123	126	102 76	
	85 122 136 142	20 105 122	122 137	31 127		80	73	136	
	31 145 21 141 146	123 46 115 137 22,81, 53	73 146	76 52 142	34 73 80 77 148 79	20 45 71 137	77 45	141 70 126 47	
	33 141 102 147	37 123 19 137	33	33 80 51,87,105	35 51 61 70	51 122 102 137		136	
	34,41,72,51 136,52,135	30 80 148	35	37 81 80	45 144	30 43 79 147	43 58 76	129 136	
	148 147	48 19 68	119 110 87	87 148	21 128 146 145	134 21 123	123 136	79 135 121,64,76	
	61 87 131	21 103 104	19	134	36 54 82 148	102 20 137,18,131		129 120 73	
	147 135 105 51	87,85,137 135,19,131	52 141	35 127 148	44 73 75,76,148	18 136 146	79 112	145 118	
52		121 133 122	103,123 92	35 118	37 87 102 122	74 122 109,103,90	130 102 90	22 71 61	
	87 144 147	46 137 54	120 33	35 132	52 76 141 142	66 123	103	136 47	
	128 35 51	32 85	123		43	64 36 123	126		
34					22	82 21			
								76	45
109									

HINTS ON USING THE CHARTS

Location is based on selecting the correct chart in priority order. If difficulty is experienced in finding a cartouche, the following may be helpful.

Check that you have selected the correct chart as follows:-

1. Look for the group signs first, from the list at the top of Chart A.
2. If no group signs are present look for the figure of Gods or Men.
3. If both group signs and figures of Gods or Men are in the cartouche use Chart A.
4. If none of the above group signs or Gods/Men are present then look for a circle in the cartouche. Then select Chart C or D, depending upon the total number of signs in the cartouche.
5. If none of the above are present then use Chart ~~D~~ E, ic., - no group signs, no Gods/Men, and no circles.

A few signs are duplicated in the same chart, thus if the intersection of the two signs does not locate the cartouche then try the other duplicate signs.

Chart E is the hardest to use since it caters for most of the Queens and others who did not have epithets in their cartouche.

Many of the hieroglyphic signs are similar in shape, so it has been necessary to compromise in the charts, eg., -

 ba (ram) =  ka (bull),  =  etc.

 ir (eye) =  r (mouth),  =  etc.

 (crocodile on stand) =  (crocodile not on stand)

To effectively utilise space on the charts, all the signs are not included, so use the sign which look the nearest in shape, and this will probably give the correct cartouche.

Please note that sometimes group signs plus God/Men, and circles, are found in the same cartouche. The priority is always Chart A - then Chart B. With a little practice you will find that the charts are easy to use.

7 ROYAL TITLES AND PREFIXES TO CARTOUCHES

The following is a list of prefixes which determine the status of the peson named in the cartouche.

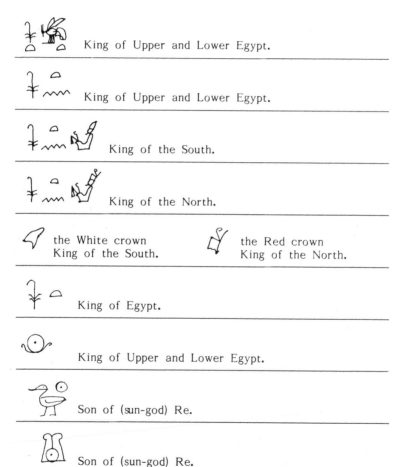

 King of Upper and Lower Egypt.

 King of Upper and Lower Egypt.

 King of the South.

 King of the North.

 the White crown
King of the South.

 the Red crown
King of the North.

 King of Egypt.

 King of Upper and Lower Egypt.

 Son of (sun-god) Re.

 Son of (sun-god) Re.

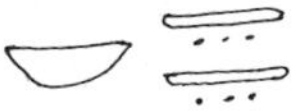 Lord of the two lands.

 Royal Wife of the king.

 King's son.

 King's daughter.

 Prince (great one).

 Princess.

 Prince.

 King's son.

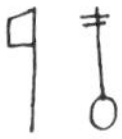 Good god (beautiful god).

 Good goddess (beautiful goddess).

 Granted life.

 Like Re.

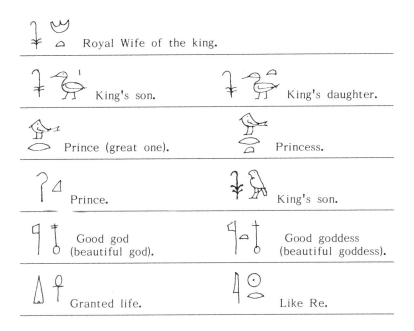

<u>**SOME EPITHETS**</u> - attached to the King's name within the cartouche.

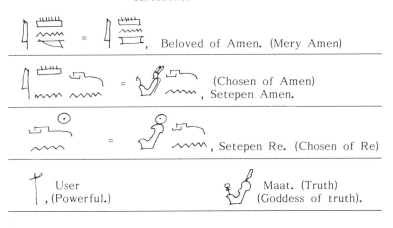

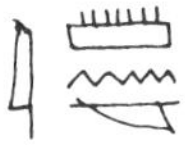 = 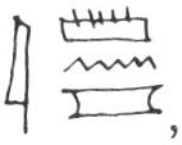, Beloved of Amen. (Mery Amen)

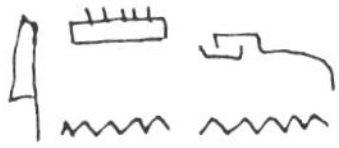 = , Setepen Amen. (Chosen of Amen)

 = , Setepen Re. (Chosen of Re)

, User (Powerful.)

 Maat. (Truth) (Goddess of truth).

10 SELECT BIBLIOGRAPHY

BAINES, J & MALEK, J Atlas of Ancient Egypt (Oxford 1980).

BECKERATH, J.V Untersuchuugen zur polischen Geneschichte det Zweiten Zwischenzeit in Agypten (Gluckstadt 1965).

BIERBRIER, M.L The Late New Kingdom in Egypt (Warminster 1975).

BRUGSCH-BEY, E Le livre des rois (Cairo 1887).

BUDGE, Sir E.A.W A History of Egypt (London 1902).
The Kings of Egypt (London 1908).
Legends of the Gods (London 1912).

DAVID, R Cult of the Sun (London 1980).

DUNHAM, D & LAMING MACADAM, F Names and relationships of the royal family of Napata JEA 45 (1949).

EMERY, W.B Archaic Egypt (Middlesex 1984).

GARDINER, Sir A Egyptian Grammar (Oxford 1982).
Egypt of the Pharaohs (Oxford 1961).
The Royal Canon of Turin.

GAUTHIER, M.H Le livre des rois d'Egypte Vol's 1-4 (Cairo 1913-15).

HOFFMAN, M.A Egypt Before the Pharaohs (London 1980).

KEES, H Ancient Egypt (Chicago and London 1961).

KITCHEN, K.A The Third Intermediate Period in Egypt (1100-650 BC). (Warminster 1973).

LEPSIUS, C.R Konigsbuch der alten Agypter (Berlin 1858).

MASPERO, G The Dawn of Civilisation, Egypt and Chaldaea (London 1910).
The Struggle of the Nations, Egypt, Syria and Assyria (London 1925).

MONTET, P Le lac sacre de Tanis (Paris 1966).
Les constructions et el Tombeau de Psousennes a Tanis. (Paris 1951).

MURRAY, M.B The Splendour that was Egypt (London 1977).

NEWBERRY, P.E Ancient Egyptian Scarabs (London 1905).

PETRIE, Sir W.M.F Scarabs and Cylinders with names (Warminster 1978).

PORTER, B & MOSS, R Bibliography of Egypt Parts 1-VII (Oxford 1927-52).

ROMER, J The Valley of the Kings (London 1981).

SHORTER, A.W The Egyptian Gods (London 1981).

WADDELL, W.G Manetho (c 1930).

WARD, W.A The Chronology of Egypt and Western Asia 2200-1900 BC (Lebanon 1971).

WINLOCK, H.E The Rise and Fall of the Middle Kingdoı at Thebes (New York 1947).

9 INDEX OF ROYAL NAMES

This index contains all the royal names used throughout the book, including:- the king's cartouche names with some variant readings commonly used, Horus names (H), Queens (Q), Princes (P), Princesses (Ps), and Gods (G). The spellings reflect the variety of renderings commonly used but others may be found elsewhere.

INCOMPLETE NAMES

EPILOGUE

Osiris is buried when the corn seed is covered by the rich black Nile earth, and is risen again when the green corn stem sprouts up.

The Egyptians never grew tired of the Osiris legend. With the passing of time the Sons of Re came and went but Osiris reigned forever. Each Egyptian lived and died believing in Osiris, they never really took to sun-worship in the same way. Osiris was their own earthly god, Re was but the mystical idol of their fleeting kings.